NOT SIMPLY BROKEN

Not Simply Broken

Betty Khalili

AceChoice Publishing and Branding

Contents

Author's Note	3
A Note from Publisher Pantea Kalhor	4
Foreword by Antonio G Scisci, Program Designer and Event Planner	6
Foreword by Majed Gharavi, PhD in Comparative Study of Religion, Teacher	7
Foreword by Sara Rahimian, B. A, M. A Realtor®	10
This Book is Dedicated to	12
Introduction	13
Chapter 1: My Life Journey from Childhood to University	16
Chapter 2: Pistachios, Me, and My Dad	33
Chapter 3: Scratched Wounds on My Heart, My Father's Death	39
Chapter 4: My Love Story, From Dating to Marriage	43
Chapter 5: My Mother and Her Big Surprise	47
Chapter 6: I Became a Mother	51
Chapter 7: Something Unexpected Shattered My Heart, My Sister, Atefeh	56
Chapter 8: Are We Moving to A Dreamland?	63

Chapter 9: That Was Not What I Expected Either! My
Separation Story   72

Chapter 10: Sama Whirling Dance for My Son's
Engagement   80

Chapter 11: I Set Myself Free, Florida Getaway   85

Acknowledgement   94

Special Thanks to My Publisher   95

About the Author, Betty Khalili   96

Photo Insert   97

Not Simply Broken
A Memoir by Betty Khalili
Gathered and Published by AceChoice Publishing and Branding
https://acechoiceidea.com

Copyright

Not Simply Broken

Copyright © 2022 by Acechoice Publishing and Branding

All Rights Reserved

ISBN-13: 978-1-7780445-2-6

No part of this publication may be used or reproduced, stored in a retrieval system,

or transmitted in any form or by any means—for example, electronic, photocopy, or

recording—or in any manner whatsoever without the prior written consent of the

author.

https://acechoiceidea.com/NotSimplyBroken

AceChoice Publishing and Branding

Author's Note

Dear Reader,

It is with great excitement and deep gratitude that I present to you my book, *Not Simply Broken*.

This book is the story of hope and resilience in which a woman encounters a journey full of unexpected twists and turns and yet continues to find her way home all over again.

Not Simply Broken is one of intuition and insight, of deep introspection, and of choosing to create new meanings in your life.

It is a tale of immense gratitude for recognizing the miracle of existence and celebrating life despite the circumstances.

To my dear readers, my one hope in writing this book is to ignite a flame within your soul, be it big or small. Whether it should take a single sentence or the book in its entirety, I hope that my story can inspire others to recreate theirs. Because life is worth it.

Betty Khalili, June 2022

A Note from Publisher Pantea Kalhor

Working with Betty was one of the most enjoyable experiences I have had in my publishing history. The moment I heard about her story; I knew I would publish this book. Because Betty was born and raised in the same country as me, I was familiar with her tale even before it was completely told. From the Iran revolution, war, immigration, to marriage and being a mother; every piece of her story resonated with me.

Betty is brilliant, a fast learner, and a high achiever. Since we started working together, her life has totally changed. She was the creator of her brand-new life. She has firmly fought and stood up for her goals and dreams despite her father's resistance and the bitter taste of infidelity in her broken marriage.

She has proven that nobody but us is responsible for our happiness. Sometimes, obeying the family rules to fit in with society may have a conflict with our goals and our plans. Sometimes, we need to cross our boundaries and fight for what we believe. It is easier to be a follower and not an initiator since you give the authority to others to manage your life. Yes, it's easier to ignore our dreams to satisfy others. But we need to see ourselves as an individual looking at our life from outside. Do you pity your life for what you could have done but didn't because you prioritized your obligations as an excuse?

Sometimes, we need to take a break and look at ourselves in the mirror. How happy and satisfied are we with what we see in the mirror?

I believe when we have passionate goals and dreams, but we suppress our desires or postpone them to eternity, we cannot feel happy.

Not Simply Broken is a great example of how fighting for dreams and staying resilient and positive can have rewarding results. Betty highlights the role of her good friend Zari as an inspiration in pursuing her education, her mother's support in the sensitive stages of her life and love of her son as a stimulus for improving her life and fighting for the better future.

Her story reflects one part of Iran's history which pinpoints behind the scenes of Iranians' lives before and after the revolution. She is also a successful paradigm of a Canadian immigrant who rebuilt her life a few times and remained loyal to her goals.

As human beings, our lives will be a mixture of happiness and sorrows. We all experience spring, summer, fall, and winter. But staying hopeful is what we need, to see the beauty in all stages of our lives. We may see a beam of light in a dark tunnel and be Not Simply Broken by any deluge or thunderstorm.

Foreword by Antonio G Scisci, Program Designer and Event Planner

Not Simply Broken, by Betty Khalili, is a wonderful book about one woman's soulful attempt to make sense of the changes in her life. Her message is to try not to shatter apart if you're in a bad situation when life is hard hitting and dismal. The memoir follows her journey from Iran to Canada, focusing on the important lessons she acquired along the way that she could not have planned or imagined.

Her candour about her life as a young child growing up to be a woman gives her story strength. She is fearless, enthralling, and supple as she confronts her own humanity, as well as ours, with all the turmoil and elegance that entails family, friends, and relationships. In this memoir, you'll meet her as an open and funny person. Her lovely words will make you laugh, weep, and smile again.

I thought this book is a realistic tale that evoked memories and feelings in me as the son of an immigrant family. The memoir is an inspirational story that demonstrates that the sacrifices we make or risks we take for those we truly love are stronger than any material object we may possess, and that we can achieve everything we wish or want through belief in ourselves.

Foreword by Majed Gharavi, PhD in Comparative Study of Religion, Teacher

This book is made up of different faces. While most biographies often revolve around life events, this book focuses on the people in the author's life. Each person has a dedicated chapter, and I believe this is the most important takeaway from the book. Our lives are ultimately shaped by the people in it, as opposed to events. The author's description of the people in her book is incredibly detailed. Sometimes I quarreled with them, sometimes I shed tears with them, and sometimes I held their hands tightly in my own... In this book, I realized how alone we truly are as humans — whether we are the oppressor or the oppressed. I also realized that the same loneliness ultimately leads to the discovery of meaning and depth in life.

Of all the characters in this book, the one that touched me the most was "Zari," a character the author only knew on a first-name basis. She tries to find her but fails. The character represents an element of mystery and renowned glory. For this reason, I would like to talk a little about Zari amongst the other characters. Perhaps because I am a teacher myself, I observed a sense of leadership and wisdom in her character, further deepening my perspective of the character. Zari is a person we all need in our lives. They are one who discovers the inanimate aspects of our lives, and whose presence is in the strength of one's heart to set foot on unknown paths. In particular, there were five traits she possessed that stood out to me.

The very first trait was that of her action-oriented approach to life. Instead of offering "positive" reassurances, she instead suggests a simple action to the author, Betty: to create a library.

Another feature I deeply resonate with is her ability to solve some of life's most difficult problems with wholehearted acceptance. In this book's instance, instead of arguing and coaxing Betty's father to let Betty go to school, she accepts this fact and finds a way to overcome the challenge. In the case of this book, she finds a time when Betty's father wasn't home to support Betty's educational journey. In a time when people want to solve their problems through negotiation, talk, and persuasion, Zari's refreshing approach consolidates the principle of working through life, akin to a river bending and accommodating around rocks and ridges, as opposed to trying to move them.

Thirdly, Zari's presence was quiet and unassuming. Despite her influence and inspiring nature, her presence did not weigh heavily on Betty's life. This point is illustrated in the duration of Betty's recent search for Zari when she had slipped away quietly in a place unbeknownst to Betty.

Another trait that stood out to me were her eyes and how they shone. While we may meet many good people in our lives, there are far fewer who, when they help us, do so with eyes that shine with enthusiasm. It is for this reason I find that oftentimes a simple look or smile can soothe a soul through life's hardship, more than a thousand tips, and well-meaning advice.

Lastly, her presence with Betty through moments of fear and hope consolidated Betty's resilience. Zari inspired her to go on despite her circumstances, making her journey one of the most empowering moments of Betty's life. Zari's unbridled activism and philosophy etched a permanent mark of courage and strength into Betty's life.

Whilst reading this book, many of you may question who or what played the role of Zari in their own lives. However, to that, I pose the more important question: "How can I be more like Zari?" The life shown in Betty's book illustrates that she sought the answer to this second question from the heart of all failures; perhaps, for this reason, life coaching is her answer to that concern.

Foreword by Sara Rahimian, B. A, M. A Realtor®

What a pleasure to be part of Betty's journey and to read her memoir, *Not Simply Broken*.

Some people cross paths in mere serendipity. Some people's souls connect with no real explanation why. I felt this way with Betty Khalili and her story hit my soul. She hit my soul. At a party in the summer, Betty walked up to me, along with her son, Abteen, heartbroken.

She told me about her spouse's infidelity. When we stood in a protected circle, I mentioned that this felt like complete déjà vu: a feeling of having already experienced the present situation. Abteen said the same thing. As if this experience was meant to happen. From that day, we developed a friendship, and I got to know Betty more. I've known Betty briefly in my life, but my soul feels like I've known Betty for a lifetime.

One beautiful afternoon at a French-inspired café, Betty and I spoke about the struggles of immigration, and the taboos within the Iranian community, from mental health to cheating. We spoke about the importance of being independent women. We spoke about energy and faith.

We spoke about our sons; Betty's son who recently got married and mine being a toddler exploring life. We were two women, sharing our hopes, dreams, struggles, and heartaches. Although we talked about struggles, what I appreciated about Betty was every conversation ended in hope and growth. The conversation was about heavy topics but light in energy if that makes sense.

Betty understands that you must go through your struggles and pains, feel them, experience them, but overcome them. She demonstrates this so well in her memoir. She touches on so many important topics in her book and I am honoured to be a small part of her journey.

As a mom, as a wife, as an entrepreneur and "boss mom" (Realtor), as an Iranian Canadian, and a person who understands and feels energy, I connected with her story. Her whimsical stories about her childhood and youth capture the readers as she takes you on a journey of immigration, marriage, and personal crisis. Betty will triumph on her journey. It has only just begun; she is not broken!

This Book is Dedicated to

This book is dedicated **to my mother, Marzieh**, who has lived a life of hardship and difficulty. Who, through loss and grief, carried the burden of raising nine children on her own. Throughout my life, she taught me about the sheer strength of a mother, and how to use life lessons as a means to learn through morals and principles. Her presence was my shelter on my darkest days, ceaselessly uplifting me with her everlasting faith. With every word of encouragement, she helped me pick up the fallen pieces and build my life up again, piece by piece. She was a woman who had every reason to protest and give up, having lived through heartbreak, grief, and hardship, yet somehow, she never did. It was at that point I learned how to stand as she did, to sometimes bend, but to never break.

To my son, **Abteen**, who has and always will be my forever love. Whose wise and gentle presence has touched many souls, including mine, with his generous and kind-hearted soul.

Introduction

Suspended in a dream world, I'm running with broken high heels. Running feels difficult and painful. There were times my feet felt as though they would fail me, and times my lungs were about to give up as I panted, gasping for air. I stood to catch my breath. I am here. But I don't know where I am.

Perhaps it is in a parallel world in which life is different. I am wearing my broken red high heels, walking with a newfound confidence; the earth and sky lie beneath my feet, and I'm lost in a cloudy tunnel of time.

I take off my shoes and start to walk along a sandy beach barefoot. Whether I have heels on or not, or whether I have any shoes on at all, it doesn't matter anymore. The sand is hot, just bearable to walk on. In the solitary blue, everything is calm. I have only brought my memories with me, and my shoes in my hands. I trudge closer to the water and ponder to myself: *"You can still play like a child in this cool water; you can still create new adventures."*

I later found a quiet place, sat on a rock, and let my soul fly away where it needed to go, to my father's library; my mother's trembling shoulders, shaken and bent under her losses and pains of raising nine children, losing both her husband and daughter, and yet having never forgotten to smile… to the happy sounds of a family reunion, after years of longing and distance. Different voices talk all together at once, giddy laughs and shrieks ensue after seeing each other together one more time.... We talk of the old days, remembering the happy and sad moments.

Oh, how much I love this life! With its never-ending shades of grays and whites, its losses, griefs, and ups and downs. How much I love the feelings of being loved and gifting love. The sense of unity — of being a mother! The depth of love while embracing my son, and simply hearing him breathe. I long to hear his sweet childish voice one more time, when he was only a toddler and just called me "Mama" for the first time. I love the feeling of beginning: migrating, moving, rebirthing, and recreating. The time has arrived for me to rebirth. I have been born one more time with every one of these pages.

Life is like ending a line, inserting a period, and starting a new line...

I polished my soul amongst the pains. I went through separation, my sister's death, and my father's death.

When immigrating, I left the half-paved road to start anew all over again... a new line.

Periods, pauses, and commas were scrawled on written lines, and I find myself creating new ones, each starting with a capital letter.

In this short time after my divorce, it feels as though I was born one more time. My intrepid soul has longed to create. I have fought endlessly; I faced difficulties of limitations, disagreements, and gender discrimination. But I could finally free myself and run over the boundaries.

Regardless of the restrictions and obstacles I faced, I was a warrior for my dreams. I celebrated with myself when no one else did.

Walking without my red high heels gives a sense of immense joy and freedom. I will walk again. I will continue to walk barefoot on the hot sand that may burn my feet, and if it does, I wade in the water yet again to cool them down.

I hope you can be a creator of your life too. I hope you experience rebirth. You might need to insert a period or a comma, pause and restart writing a new line or a new chapter... But life is worth it.

Period. New line. New chapter.

Why I Wrote This Book?

Over the years, my closest friends, my only child, and some of my colleagues encouraged me to write about my life. Recent events in my life took me to very dark days and made me struggle to find a way to survive. Writing became my way to overcome the pain, and that was how the book was formed.

Chapter 1: My Life Journey from Childhood to University

The family doctor checked my throat and asked me to say "AAH". I looked at my older sister who was watching us, and thought to myself, *"You are the next. Maybe you get to be poked by a big ampule in your butt."* Dad sat on a chair in the doctor's office looking worried. I said, "AAH," and swallowed my saliva with pain. I looked at the doctor's eyes with my innocent childish look and, in my mind, begged him not to prescribe any injections. It was so common that for each simple flu or small headaches, Dad would take us to this neighborhood doctor who knew all our family members. I guess he liked my dad a lot since we were a big family and Dad was always worried about us. We were a good income source for him. After the appointment, my dad took us to the drugstore across the street from the doctor's office and filled out the prescriptions for me and my sister. There were no injections this time. I was relieved, but as always, the plastic bag in my dad's hands containing one of those bitter cough syrups looked scary. We came home and Dad complained to Mom that my sister wasn't answering the doctor's questions and kept quiet all the time. I was proud that I could answer each question the doctor asked me very politely. There were plenty of visits with this doctor, as far back as I remembered, for small and tiny problems. Dad and the doctor had a strong bond and trusted each other completely.

When my younger siblings were born, I remember seeing Dad anxious all the time. If one of them cried a lot overnight, he would take the kid to the doctor first thing in the morning, questioning a lot and demanding a thorough examination. People told him this was just how kids were, but he couldn't help it.

My mom had never married anyone else before my dad. She was much younger than him. He was married before, though. Despite the fact he desperately wanted kids, he hadn't had a chance with his two previous wives. I wonder if maybe that was the reason. He was so worried all the time about our well-being that even a common flu would scare him to the point where he spent a lot of money taking us to see his trusted physician.

Our family culture taught us that boys were more valuable than girls. Boys would help take care of the family and business. They would provide. But girls were different. Many families preferred to have boys because they thought girls would just get married and leave home and couldn't contribute to the family's income. We had seven girls and two boys, and my dad loved each of us so much. Regardless of his concerns for all of us, he always gave more credit to his sons' educations and desires. On the other hand, he created overprotective restrictions for his daughters in a way that he thought was caring.

When, after six girls, my mom gave birth to a baby boy, the news was spread so rapidly in our neighborhood. Everyone was so excited. People in the neighborhood's mosque were over the moon and said the special "Thanksgiving prayers" nonstop. The excitement affected us as kids, too. I was 10 years old and the fourth kid in my family. My dad was ecstatic, and I did not remember ever before seeing him as happy as he was when my brother was born. The smile did not leave my mom's face. We all cherished this new baby boy in our household and embraced him in our arms. If he cried overnight, my dad would pick him up and would walk him in our alley, pacing up and down in the middle of the night to calm the baby. In the meantime, Mom had a chance to rest. For days and nights after his birth, our house was full of people coming with sweets to congratulate my parents. The happiness sat in each corner of the house. My sisters and I would fight each other, whose turn it was to hug or change him. Not long after, my second brother was born. My parents' wishes were fulfilled again, and they were beyond happy. Their last kid was a girl, and, before her birth, my mom asked my dad's permission to go for C-section and end her ability to have more children by tying her tubes. Surprisingly, Dad agreed, and that was the end of Mom's pregnancies, although she was only 40 when my youngest sister was born.

The differences between girls and boys in our family were so obvious; boys could get everything, and girls were forced to stay at home after grade five. I could see the sexism, which really bothered me. When my second brother was born, my mom was over the moon since she felt complete as a woman. Back then, if you couldn't have a boy, the blame was on the woman. She would put the blame on herself that she couldn't carry a boy, and society agreed.

In Iran, elementary school was up to grade five. In my family's culture, girls were allowed to attend school up to that point. Because my father didn't believe in sending girls to school any longer, regardless of how interested or how smart they were, he decided that my sisters had to stop attending school after fifth grade. My sisters were so smart that people tried to convince my dad to let them continue schooling, but that did not happen. Instead, they had to take sewing classes and learn how to be a good housewife and a mother. Our jobs would be to care for the kids, clean them, nurse them, feed them, and change diapers, and nothing more. I loved elementary school, though, and I wanted to stay in school forever.

In my last year of elementary school, there was a revolution in our country. Everything was changing, and I had to stay home like my sisters. While I was doing housework, my mind wandered elsewhere. I was thinking about school.

The Islamic revolution shifted everything, even, attitudes about girls going to school. I had hoped that things might get better. Revolution and protesting happened on the streets, and when my 15-year-old sister and her fiancé went to the demonstrations, 11-year-old me tagged along. My sister had a bit more freedom in public. If she was with her fiancé, our dad relaxed some of his rules.

I found myself curious about the protests and demonstrations. I started to learn more things on my own. I borrowed books from famous Iranian authors: Shariat, Hedayat, Jalal Al Ahmad, Simin Daneshvar...

My parents encouraged us to attend the mosque in our neighborhood. They wanted us to learn about religion and pray. We were going to mosque regularly, but we didn't pray; we met with a bunch of other girls there and mosque was a safe place to chit-chat. We talked about every subject, especially boys and how babies were born. I remember one of my older sisters couldn't stop crying when she found out how babies were made.

"No, no, my dad with my mom, it's impossible?!!! It's a lie. They wouldn't do such a thing," she sobbed.

"So, how do you think you got to the world?" one of the naughtier girls asked her.

"Oh! By the way, I think your parents were doing it more than our parents. Look how many of you were born." Another girl interrupted.

"My dad would not ever do such a thing with my mom! God gave us to them," my sister insisted.

I was smaller, only 12 or 13 years old, and the news shocked me too. But I accepted it as it was and counted nine kids. So, they did it nine times. It was not that horrible!

The nights at the mosque were fun for us. Even though we cared less about prayers, we were eager to go there and continue our discoveries.

A gorgeous friend of ours read my palm in the mosque. "You will travel a lot; I see you on airplanes. You are going far away from here and will live in a very distant place. Your husband's name starts with M and you're going to have two kids." In my mind, I thought about all the boy's names that started with M. We girls sat in a circle, whispering and giggling. Our fortune-telling friends would take turns reading everyone's palms. Some older ladies looked at us with blame and regret, as we weren't serious about praying. They noticed that every night, we had secret meetings in the mosque.

The palm reading for me somehow came out right, although we didn't believe in her at the time and were just doing it for fun. In my mind, the farthest place I could ever live was east of Iran and less than 1000 km from Tehran, where my eldest sister lived. This palm reader was a free girl with big black eyes and Persian-looking eyebrows. Her hair was so black and silky that I always wanted to touch it. She was always happy and laughed so hard all the time. She was our fun and naughty friend and somehow the head of all meetings. I wish I could see her again and tell her that her palm reading came true. She, her sister, and their family stayed in our neighborhood for only one year and moved out too soon.

My second sister, Zahra, was the one who suffered the most as a girl. The first sister got lucky and got engaged to a man to whom my aunt - from my father's side - introduced her when she was in her teens. She loved her husband, and he loved her back. They moved to the east of the country and built their life together. This made my parents think that all of us girls would marry in our teens before we turned 16. It was hard for the second girl since she wasn't as obedient as the first one. She had big dreams and was stubborn. I remember we both went to our neighborhood mosque to practice meditations and theatre. After the revolutions, mosques became cultural and activity locations. Young people gathered to sing Islamic songs together and play theatres. I was 12 or 13 and four years younger than my second sister. I wasn't fully involved in activities in the mosque, but she was. Since she had finished her elementary school and wasn't allowed to continue school, she got more involved in these activities. I remember one day we were practicing hypnotism, and we laid down in a circle on the floor. Our instructor was so good and used our imaginations to take us to the north of Iran to a rice field (SHALYZAR) and gave us breathing exercises. After he counted backward, we couldn't wake up my sister. I was so scared: what if she stayed in the rice field forever and didn't wake up at all? Years later, I was watching the 2010 movie "Inception," and it caught my attention when Leonardo DiCaprio's wife didn't want to come back to their real world anymore. I was reminded of this childhood memory of my sister.

There was another day at practice when my other sister showed up with a letter in her hand and gave it to my instructor. I was a kid, and they wouldn't let me get involved in more grown-up things. I learnt later that the letter was from my dad to my older sister, Zahra, asking if she was going to marry one of the boys in our neighborhood who used to be our neighbor. His mom kept calling my sister her daughter-in-law for years, and then one day she was at our home with her son, asking for my dad's permission for the two to marry.

My sister didn't like that family at all and didn't want to marry him. She told me later that she was so scared to write back, "No," she didn't know what to do. They had to stop theater practice for her… The director came to her questioning what was holding her back from returning to class?

She showed the letter from my dad.

He asked, "What's your answer to this question?"

"No is my final answer," she mumbled shyly.

The director banged the pen on the desk loudly, and exclaimed, "I count to ten and by 10 you have to write your answer. One… two… three…" He banged the pen on the desk with each number.

My sister thought, "By saying no, I will be in big trouble and will get punished. By saying yes, I would marry this man who I don't like at all…"

The countdown continued: four… five… six… seven…

Someone reminded her it was getting late, and everyone was waiting for her.

The director was looking at his watch, still counting. "Eight… nine…"

And my sister wrote a big NO on the paper with my dad's handwriting on it.

This was insane, mad, and dangerous.

We went back home. Everything looked so normal. The boy and his mother were still upstairs in our guest room. My sister was shocked and found out the letter reached only my mom, who never dared to give it to my dad.

She told my sister, "We all need to be obedient and follow our father's advice. It's right for us."

We should only listen to our parents since they know what is best for us. The boy's mom came downstairs and gave my sister a watch as a symbol of their engagement. The watch was too big, and she said she would return it to fix the size. My sister was certain she would not marry this guy, and she never did, despite of all troubles she faced. Years later, they managed to get my third sister to marry the same son, who was still single.

One Friend Can Change Your Whole Life Forever

When we desperately look for a change, we send signals to the universe. Right people and right opportunities appear on our way. There are always signs around you that you should not ignore. Angels are real. They come to help you in different forms; so, embrace them.

The universe heard my prayer, my fervent desire to go to school and continue my education.

My sister, Zahra, had a friend who was an activist. They were both 4 years older than me. Zari was optimistic, open-minded, and an avid reader. She and I formed a friendship and the more I got to know her, the more I loved her and wanted to be like her. Through our conversations, she encouraged me to build a small neighborhood library.

Her family was so different from mine. Her mom was divorced and lived with someone else, which was unusual for me. There were three girls in her family, Zari being the oldest. She had dreams of attending medical school and I wondered if that would be possible for me, too. It was a far-reaching dream, but we started small with this neighborhood library. We added to it and shared books. Zari wanted me to go back to school next year, but I told her it was impossible. I stayed home one full year after grade five; I was 11 or 12 years old and missed the school so much, I couldn't bear not going back to school for the rest of my life.

She was surprised. "Look how many different books you have read in the past year. You are a genius."

When the next school year started, kids were excited to go back to school, but I just sat in our small room with the radio. There was a song that played each year: "Hello classmates, hello classmates, we are coming back to see you. Are you coming back to classes?"

A lump formed in my throat, and I burst into tears. I didn't understand why I couldn't go back to school. I read a lot of books. I wanted to be a doctor, a dentist, maybe even a lawyer. All I knew was that I desperately wanted to go to school, but my dad wouldn't let me.

Zari tried to encourage me to return to school and said she would help me, but that would go against everything my father stood for. He wouldn't allow it. The once exciting welcome back song on the radio now sounded sad to me since I was not going to join my classmates.

One grey fall afternoon, Zari knocked on the door, her arms overloaded with books. My mom opened the door as Zari said, "Let me in, I am about to drop these books."

She smiled so brightly, and her eyes shone as she rushed inside the house. "I am sending you back to school."

My mom and I stared at her in shock. She was insane! I was excited about this, but scared, too. Zari said she tried to come over the other day, but she heard my dad from outside and returned without ringing the bell.

She was here again, and she would like to study with me. She would teach me. It wasn't happening the way I thought it would or wanted, but Zari was going to homeschool me. I'd never heard of that before, but she said she would register me for exams, and this way I could learn as much as I wanted. Years later, she finished medical school, married her sweetheart, and moved to Canada and later to the US. I tried so hard to find her. She had mentioned earlier that she didn't like her last name, so I believe that was the reason she was not searchable. I couldn't even find her family since they had moved to different countries!

I studied at home without my dad knowing. When it came time for exams, Zari would come and pick me up with some excuse, like going to hang out or heading to the mosque. But we would go so I could write my exam. Those days, those challenges, crying and swinging between hope and despair, were some of the strongest in my memory.

Finally, when schools became separated by gender, I was able to attend high school in person. There were three years of middle school and four of high school. It used to be those schools with mixed gender, but after the Iranian revolution, the schools were separated. My dad agreed to let me go to an all-girls high school.

Academic Competition among high schools

I did excellent in high school. I was not only at the top in my class and school but also in the whole region among boys and girls both.

In my second year of high school, I was nominated to compete in an academic knowledge competition against other students from the city where I lived. Nobody accompanied me or supported me; I went alone. I took the bus, changing buses a few different times to get to where I needed to be. The competition was in a large arena, and when I arrived, I saw kids everywhere with their parents. I thought I was the only one there without someone to cheer me on.

As I look at the surrounding people, I saw they were dressed well and carried books and lots of supplies with them. I was dressed plainly and had only a pencil, eraser, and pencil sharpener. I felt out of place with these kids. They all had years of schooling and they knew how academic competition worked. I learned at home for so many years, I barely even called myself a high schooler. These kids didn't know their privilege to have spent so much time with their friends at school. I worried that I didn't stand a chance here. I couldn't win this competition. I couldn't beat them. They were all so much better prepared.

Then, I reminded myself that I might be different, but I had spent years working to this point. I believed in myself, I dreamed, I worked hard. And my school chose me for this competition. What did I have to lose by trying? Nothing. I might not win. I might not even do very well, but if I did my best, that was enough. I sat for the test and the questions confused me. I was not sure if I understood them correctly because they seemed too easy. I answered the best I could and when I finished, I turned in my paper. I was the first one done and was not sure if that was a good sign or bad. Then I had to wait.

I went back home and waited for the results. The morning of the announcement, every student at school was gathered in the yard. We stood, exercised, prayed, sang, and listened to the announcements. I was surprised when the principal called my name. I won. I was in shock and couldn't believe it! I had won and was number one in academics out of all those girls and boys in the whole region.

The principal handed me the prize and exclaimed, "We're first in the region. We are so proud of you!"

At home that day, I announced my win to my mother. She was so proud and happy and hugged me very tightly.

One year after the Iranian revolution, open warfare between Iran and Iraq began in September 1980. People had to learn how to defend themselves and their country. There were different workshops on how to practice working with guns, how to neutralize a bomb, or how to defend ourselves.

Me, Zari, and my sister started going to shooting class together. They taught us different tactics of how to defend ourselves in case of getting arrested by the enemy. We had to open and close a Kalashnikov rifle or Machine Pistole (MP) in one minute. We were anxious and stressed to follow the instructions properly. The instructor served in the military and was really serious about what he taught. There was no place for laughs or jokes. I was young and scared of war, death, or becoming a hostage. We heard a lot of horrible stories about the cities close to the border where women were raped and had to flee their homes while their men were at the center of the war, being killed, injured, or captured.

Those days were dark and horrific. Sometimes I could see horror in Zari's eyes; however, at the same time, she tried to buoy everyone up with her cheerful and energetic spirit. On the contrary, I was furious, uncertain of the future of my country, and afraid of losing my life and my loved ones. One day, her eyes looked different. I could find a trace of happy glitter in her eyes, a hidden sign of good news or an annunciation.

"What is the matter with you? It looks like you're flying on top of clouds." I told her, while tilting my head and looking at her.

She laughed hard and looked at me with a bright face: "I just got married one hour before I came to the workshop!!!"

I was speechless! How is that even possible?

She was a young, beautiful girl who was ambitious and clever enough to have the most exciting wedding ever! And spend the night with her husband, not with us in shooting class. I didn't understand her.

"The ceremony was very simple. I didn't even have a wedding gown or anything special. There was only the immediate family, and this is my honeymoon!" she said with a warm laugh.

I admire her now even more. She was a hero to me, and I wanted to be just like her one day.

A few years later, I was at university, and she asked me to help her niece with her school while she was going to Mecca with her husband. It was the time for me to make it up to her and show her my appreciation. I traveled all the way to her apartment in the rich part of Tehran and did my best preparing her niece for her exams. Everything worked out in the best way. Her niece passed her exams with good marks, and I was proud I did something for my role model and hero.

My proud Radio Contest

Because of my success in the academic competition, my school nominated me for another contest. The radio show had a large audience. It was a national favorite radio show called "Friday Morning with You" and broadcasted every Friday morning at 9:00 a.m. My father used to listen to this comedic and happy show. For this competition, two girls competed against two boys for the prize.

The radio station was on *Jameh-Jam* Street in the north of Tehran–the residences of the wealthy people. I didn't have proper clothing or shoes for this. How was I going to be present in this rich area? My school hired a car for me, my teammate, and a few teachers. It looked so strange to me, the girls against boys!

The show's host was famous and well-loved. He had a lot of influence in our community. Excitement filled me as we got through the show, and I could hear my heart beating the whole time. When he asked questions, we would have to be alert and ready to ring the bell. My partner and I were amazing. One question after another, we rang the bell. The boys stared at us in surprise as we answered the questions, and the audience clapped, cheered, whistled, and shouted for us.

With each question we got right, I felt more excited. The crowd cheering for us gave me strength and courage. I was so proud of myself and my partner. Eventually, we answered the final question. We got it right. We won! I was over the moon with happiness and couldn't wait to get back home and share this excitement with my family. I did it again!

In 1982, when this competition took place, there was no Internet. My family didn't have television either, because my dad believed there were often scenes which were inappropriate and destructive for kids. Even the radio was carefully regulated and because of our religion, we were not allowed to listen to the music.

The radio show was recorded instead of broadcasting live, so I had to wait a few weeks to sit and listen to the show with my family. I had held my secret about the outcome until then. Finally, I could prove to my dad that I was capable and smart, and I could win. I anxiously turned up the radio, calling to my family, "Listen, it has just started!"

Everyone gathered in the room to listen to the radio. The host announced the competitors: the two girls from my school, and the two boys. My dad winced.

"I did not know you were in this competition with boys." His voice was angry.

I didn't expect this to be a problem. I wanted to make him proud, so what was it that I had done wrong? It seemed for many years that no matter what I did, my dad never cared. My ears and cheeks flushed with shame. Then I wondered what it was I had to be ashamed of? The audience clapped and cheered. We won. He should be proud, but he was not.

I felt my own excitement fade. Winning didn't matter anymore. It wasn't enough for my dad. I gave the prize to my mother, who had always supported me. She was honored to have me.

I Finally Made It to University

My father was completely against the idea of me attending university after high school, but my mother tried to convince him otherwise. Even high school was too much for him and we never knew from one day to the next if he was going to let me go to school. Every so often, he'd decide I couldn't go to school anymore. I'd cry for days until he'd change his mind. Everyone at school knew about my situation. They knew that I might not be there. Every day was a struggle. I never knew if I could go to school or not.

Two of my teachers – religion and literature – came to our house to convince my dad to let me go to school. They begged, but he was manipulative and humiliating. He didn't like that his daughter was going to school, doing well, and striving for success. But I continued to go to the library to read books he wouldn't approve of. I read books outside of our religion, which my father wouldn't even begin to understand. Reading books outside of Islam was strictly forbidden. My father was not just religious, he was a clergyman. He lectured the people on how to be a good Muslim and about Islam. Religion was everything to him.

My teachers told him how brilliant and smart I was, that it would be a shame if I didn't finish school. They finally convinced him that I was a good girl and didn't get into things I shouldn't at school. I studied and worked hard. I had a strong personality and was not influenced by others' behaviors. He finally agreed that I could finish high school, but I still had to do everything at home as if I wasn't at school all day. I had to cook, clean, do the dishes, and care for the smaller kids. When I finished high school, I wanted to attend medical school, but my literature diploma was not enough to get me there. I needed a diploma in natural science. I felt hopeless and devastated.

Life was so different for boys. Boys could go to school, the swimming pool, and soccer or any other activities they liked. My dad was determined to provide everything for them. He hired a private driver to take them to different classes, but we girls had to stay at home and sacrifice our life just to learn how to be a good housewife. I was totally against sexism; that was an obvious discrimination, prioritizing boys' needs over girls'. That's why I could not agree with what was happening around me. As a matter of fact, I hated spending endless hours doing house chores; I hated doing dishes, ironing, and sewing. We were a big family, and the housework occupied my whole day. I would love to study, to become a doctor, a lawyer, or maybe a judge; someone who could make a difference. I was thirsty for learning new things, that was the reason I loved our little library, and I was eager to go to libraries and read books. I would like to be a scientist or a researcher. At that time, I didn't know exactly what I wanted to be, but I knew I wanted to be well-educated and earn my university degree. I knew this was not something that my father planned for me, but I wanted to follow my heart. I had a burning desire to go to university, even if this was not something common in our family or for my parents. Girls in our society were not supposed to have these skills and privileges.

Secretly, I started studying to get ready for the university exam against my father's wishes. I would pretend that I was reading the Quran. That was the holiest book for Muslims and that was the only book that my dad approved. But hidden in the middle of the Quran, I had my books from school. I read them through the night, so my dad wouldn't find out that I was studying.

I still had to keep up with the housework, so he had no excuse to be after me and would let me spend some time with myself. I did quite well at school and appreciated every minute of it. When I was happy at school, everyone could tell, including my father. He didn't like that I was happy and enjoying my life and that is when he decided I couldn't go to school.

He said, "Enough! Enough! You're not going."

Then there was a fight between my parents. My mother wanted me to continue my education; she wanted me to be happy, she wanted me to be successful, but she had no voice. She couldn't tell my dad, "No," because it would make him angry.

I struggled to learn by myself. There was no Internet, no computer, often no books to guide me. I wasn't even allowed to go to the library. I remember one day when I came home from the library, he confronted me.

"Where were you?" he demanded.

"The library."

He slapped my face, and my ear rang so loudly I thought I lost my hearing.

"You should never have been at the library. You will not leave this house anymore. You will stay home from now on."

I apologized but was heartbroken. How could I continue my education if I couldn't go to the library? I couldn't go to high school. I wanted to go to university, but that was seemingly impossible.

I had always wanted to go to medical school, but my high school diploma in literature meant that was not possible. My friend, Zari, encouraged me to go back to school for one more year so I could earn a science diploma, too.

As it turns out, the age-old adage is true: always follow your heart and never ignore your dreams.

Times were changing and my father's views softened some. My younger sisters were starting high school without any fight from my father. I knew things weren't going to be easy for them, but it wouldn't be as hard as it had been for me. There was more freedom here for women, and I thought about what I needed to do. I talked to my father and told him that I needed to go back to high school for one more year. He agreed.

I fought hard that year, reading things I'd never heard of before like math, physics, science. I didn't know anything about these subjects and crammed a four-year study into one year. But like the competitions before, I did it. I won.

One more obstacle stood before me: the university entrance exam. The competition was rough. My scores weren't good enough for medical school, but I could get into nursing school. My friends and my mother were so proud. My father was not.

"Nursing?" he said. "Nursing! Oh boy, I am so ashamed of myself. I am so ashamed of my daughter. Why would you choose nursing? Why don't you study philosophy, or something related to religion or our family culture?"

I thought by studying nursing I could be in a medical field. It was close to my dream and far better than I imagined I could achieve. I could accept this future.

But Zari told me to wait. "Don't tell your dad. Go and pretend you're going to university, but instead study more. Take the exam again. Get into medical school next year."

I was so exhausted, though. I was tired of fighting, of studying in secret. I just wanted to get to university. This was freedom. That freedom took me to nursing school. However, I had also learned by now that today's problems belong to today; they won't last forever.

Nursing was a four-year program and I realized early on that I was going to need money. My parents wouldn't give me any money because my dad was still too prejudiced against my education. Mom tried to convince him to help and support me, but with no success.

I took the plunge and got my driver's license. It was one more thing my dad disapproved of, but I felt courageous and strong. I learned how to drive. I was grateful that my mother and sisters supported me.

While I studied full time at university, I worked part time in the hospital and took the driving lessons. It took me four attempts to earn my driver's license, but at age 19, I could drive. It finally seemed like there was light at the end of the tunnel.

My mom told my dad, "She's so smart. She's capable. She can do it and you must trust her. Just trust her. She knows what she's doing."

My dad finally said Okay. He decided to buy a car so I could drive them places when they needed, partly because he was tired of hiring drivers or using public transportation. He finally realized that I could help the family. With eleven of us, it was hard to get around. He considered buying me a car until a man in our neighborhood asked him, "What happens if she gets a flat tire? What if she gets pulled over?" He pointed out that I was a young girl and not a boy. It was dangerous, and I should not want to drive alone. I fought hard to not get myself stuck in the tunnel while chasing the light.

My dad changed his mind and no longer wanted to buy me a car. It was just another disappointment. It wasn't all gloom and doom; as it turns out, disappointments give you courage to fight for what you want.

Chapter 2: Pistachios, Me, and My Dad

Pistachios smell like my childhood. Around August, my memory travels to the pistachio festival in *Damghan*, Iran. I recall long and hot summer days curling up beside my dad and dreaming big, looking through the window facing our backyard. After lunch, naps were his favourite thing. They were mine, too. When I was beside him, I felt secure and calm; it looked like nothing could bother me, not even the worst earthquake.

He was asleep, but I couldn't rest since I was very excited to attend the pistachio festival. Kids played outside in the garden, and I loved to join them. On the other hand, I didn't want to lose the peace of resting beside my father. I loved laying there forever. The security, comfort, and the warmth of his body, all these feelings were good. Despite all his rigidity towards raising his kids, especially his daughters, he was kind, compassionate, and caring.

My dad moved to the capital of Iran (Tehran) at a very young age. He lost his dad when he was only 12 years old. As the eldest son, he had to take care of his mom, his five sisters, and two brothers. Life had made him tough, overcautious, and responsible. At 12, he started working on the railway collecting small stones for the railway project going from Tehran to the east of the country, Mashhad. His family lived in a part of Semnan Province in the east of Iran, a small city in a hot and windy village called *Damghan*. They were located at a place which had only five families. Called *Nuo*, meaning "new fort," it was a lovely, historical, and mysterious fort.

Every summer we used to go there with big suitcases and belongings to spend a part of summer there. *Ghale Nuo* was famous for its *Senjed* fruit (Oleaster, Russian olives) and pistachio trees. We had five different gardens there. One was for pistachios, one was pomegranate, the others were a mix of other fruits such as different kinds of grapes, plums, and more. Each garden had a wooden door with a big wooden key. As a child, that reminded me of a mysterious gate to the garden in children's stories where you could be lost in rampant fruit trees. It was fascinating to me to hold those big wooden keys in my small hands and try to put the keys in a hole built in the wall, click the lock, and enter the mystery.

When we arrived at the fort, the sound of running water from an eye-catching wide stream was welcoming and soothing. We would pass the garden alley. Each garden had been confined with short walls. We could see the branches of the pistachio trees from the alleys. We were taught not to touch or pick them if they came out of neighbors' gardens since they did not belong to us. In Islam, they say it is robbery from neighbors; they call it *Haram*, meaning forbidden. We had enough of them anyway. All five gardens were left for my dad's family when his dad passed away. His sisters lived there, and they took care of the gardens. We would always go at the time of the pistachio festival to pick pistachios from trees, get them skinned, dry them, and bring some back home.

It was a huge, busy, and exciting festival. As kids, we used to work and play and jump among the pistachio trees. Adults laughed and told jokes and stories while holding big blankets under the trees and waiting for someone to shake the branches and drop the pistachios on the blanket.

To go inside the fort, someone had to come and open the big double gate for us from inside. My youngest aunt was married to a very old man. They lived in the first house in the fort. A rich person owned the large garden at the back of their home, and they cared for it. It was called *Bagh Shazde*, meaning "Prince's Garden," with long, stunning pathways, tall green trees, and lots of grapes, pomegranates, and pistachio trees. My favourite trailer was inside the garden, and I loved to sit there and listen to birds chirping while daydreaming.

My youngest aunt was the kindest. Days were hot and dry, and nights were cool and pleasant there. She used to entertain us with long, mysterious, and magical stories, which we loved, and kept asking her to tell us more. She was illiterate, as all my aunts were, but she could tell the most amazing long stories on those lengthy, dark summer nights, which I remembered years after and repeated them to my own son when he was born. One was a story of seven girls living with their mom in an old castle when a wandering man knocked on the castle gate. The girls made a good dinner for him and invited him to stay overnight, hoping he would marry one of them.

Outside of my dad's childhood home, there was a big stone rock where 20 people could sit just beside the stream, under the tall *Senjed* tree. That spot was our afternoon hang-out. Adults would talk and smoke hookah while skinning the pistachios. In my dad's family, gossiping was forbidden. They strongly believed that gossiping was as discreditable as eating their brother's corpse. Lying was a big sin, and they all made certain they were on time saying their prayers and fasting in Ramadan.

Every morning at five, we had to wake up and go to each garden to collect the grapes and pistachios. Usually, the pomegranates weren't ready in the summer. I loved watching the new pomegranates on trees and wished to be able to come back in fall and pick them. I still feel the freshness of the early morning air, walking with my aunts into gardens, the sound of water running from the brooks, and hearing the sheep herd going with their shepherd to green fields. I loved the scene of reconciliation between humans and nature. There was no extra noise of streets, cars, or sirens. Only birds, crickets, sheep herds, and cows might be heard.

My aunts were all so kind, peaceful, and good to animals and nature. They loved my dad because he was their older brother who took care of them and their mother after their dad passed away. My dad always sent them money and made sure they were doing okay. He would watch for their health and well-being from long-distance.

He hired some people to take care of the gardens, water them on time, and take care of all lands and the whole fort. His youngest brother had been burned in an accidental fire when they were young, and he was wheelchair bound since. His other brother had died at a very young age from tuberculosis. One loss after another had stored at his cellular level along with the burden of his primary family, his wife, and his nine kids.

All his siblings had their own ups and downs, and they shared their joy and sorrow together. Trauma, hardship, and the memory of loss and grief made my dad the way he was. Now that I think about all my childhood, I realize he just tried to protect his girls in his own way; he didn't know better. He was responsible for his big family at the age of 12, and he took good care of them until he died. How strong a man could be to carry all these burdens. With all the protective restrictions and rules in our house, he did a great job of raising us and teaching us the virtues of a good and moral life and I am always grateful for having him.

This became a foundational concept for me. I always told myself: don't judge people based on their appearance or their hasty actions. You don't know what's beneath each person's childhood history. Many behaviours originate from our thought processes or learned behaviours in childhood. There is always a reason or a whole set of reasons behind each action or decision. Try to see it from that particular person's viewpoint.

We all knew that he sent some of his income to his sisters in the village. Every year we would go there, and he'd take care of every small thing in *Ghale Nuo*. He was well respected there, and everyone talked about him with such honour and respect. Everyone from far and near knew how hard he had worked and how much he had sacrificed to take care of his loved ones.

Having two big families and carrying a huge responsibility at a very young age wouldn't make a human soft or flexible. I didn't know how to react to his rigidity and his rules. I could only fight for my dreams. There was no communication other than disagreement and fighting. I was positive that he loved each of us dearly, but he didn't know how to show it better. How would he learn any soft skills and the right way of communication? All he did was work so hard to bring bread to the table. His beliefs and ideas were the ones he was taught. Now, more than 30 years after his death, I cannot take the time back; I cannot stop fighting with him; all I can do is remember him as a great person who was so selfless and dedicated all his life to support others.

I have a vivid image in my mind while remembering him: a man with glasses in the shelter of his busy room with books, pen, and paper to write notes from his readings.

More than half of my dad's room was filled with books. The big bookcase was filled to the brim. He had them stacked on the shelves, floor, and beside his bed. He was always reading. The books were mostly in Arabic and about Islam, philosophy, and Faghih - religious jurisprudence. I always admired the bookcase and that room. I was wondering how he was able to read all of them. He used to write down notes in columns on pages in his unique handwriting. Both his Farsi and Arabic handwriting were extraordinary. As a kid, I wished I could have a room full of books for myself.

Sometimes when he wasn't home, I went to upstairs, sneaked in his room, grabbed his eyeglasses, and took the heaviest book and pretended to read... although I couldn't understand even one word of it.

When I was in my early teens, one New Year's Eve, my dad asked us to choose what we wanted as a gift for the New Year. It wasn't common for him to buy us gifts; for some reason, he wanted to that year. I only remember right before the New Year he had gone to Mecca and when he came back, he was more spiritual and attentive than usual.

My sisters requested a piece of gold, and he took them to the jewelry store and got a piece for each. I, on the other hand, wanted to have a bookcase as big as his, and requested that. Everyone looked at me as if I was out of my mind. However, Dad talked to a fine carpenter in our neighborhood and asked him to build a wooden bookcase from scratch for me. Years later, when I got married, I took it with me to my new home, but since it was too big, it didn't fit our apartment and I had to take it back to my mom's. For many years, Dad joked that my gift had become way more expensive than my sisters' gold.

At the time, I wasn't sure what the future had in store for me, but gradually I learned to trust my instincts, and trust that the universe will offer the best for me. Now I tell my loved ones: you might not see it now, but open your heart to love, be able to forgive, and embrace the beauty of life. Karma is real and it's true what they say, "What goes around, comes around."

Chapter 3: Scratched Wounds on My Heart, My Father's Death

Help, help! Please come downstairs immediately!!! I heard my mom screaming from downstairs while I was getting ready to go to the hospital for my practicum. I was supposed to present a lecture in front of my professor and classmates. It was noon and the presentation was scheduled for 2:00 p.m. I rushed downstairs, taking three steps in one. At the base of the stairs, I was shocked. I saw my dad holding his chest; he had turned purple and was gasping for air. My mom panicked as she stood there, helpless. My dad was 63 at the time of his heart attack. He had not been feeling well for several weeks, and I had taken him to the hospital to run some tests and EKGs.

He was in bed most of the time, but that morning he decided to get up and go out. Later, we found out he went to every single grocery, butcher, and bread store in the neighborhood. He had talked and chatted with every single small store owner that morning and carried on from one person to another, asking how they were doing. He came home at noon to get ready for his noon prayers.

Unexpectedly, he felt a sudden pain in his chest, tried to grab the wall, but had to sit. I found him lying down on the floor looking blue and trying to gasp for air and unable to talk. I started CPR and mouth-to-mouth breathing.

"Go tell the neighbor to bring his car," I screamed, while crying and performing CPR. I didn't see my mom rush outside. She came back with our neighbor, a guy who had a Persian rug store next to his house across the street from ours. He was speechless.

I insisted, "Let's take him to the hospital now!"

We loaded my dad into the car with the help of the neighbor and another young man we didn't know. My mom rode up front, and we sat in back with my dad. I don't even remember how we carried him. I just remember his head on my lap while I continued to perform CPR and rescue breathing. It was a useless effort in that position, but I tried to show the young man how to do compressions. Even though my dad took his last breath before we reached the hospital, his head resting in my lap, I never gave up. We pulled to the emergency entrance, where I loudly called out for a stretcher. Two security guards brought one to us. I was familiar with the hospital because this was where I'd worked for a year while studying at university, so I pushed the stretcher into the building. I called for help as though I was the nurse on duty: "We have a heart attack patient. Bring the crash cart!"

The doctor and nurses rushed towards us with the crash cart, and I'd forgotten my role as the patient's daughter – I wanted to help them get the drugs. My hands were shaking, and my voice was broken, but loud.

The doctor took his pulse and looked at me: "He's long gone."

"NO!" I insisted. "He's not. Continue with CPR! Push EPI."

They looked at me sadly and sympathetically. The doctor ordered them to continue and injected EPI directly into my dad's heart. After God knows how long, they stopped. I found myself sitting on the floor looking at my dad, lying on the stretcher. His chest, neck and face were purple. He was gone.

I looked at the young doctor and whispered, "I'm sure I broke his ribs, I heard it!!" I felt terrible saying that.

"I'm sure he didn't feel it. He was long gone. It was unavoidable. We all have done that with CPR," the doctor tried to empathize with me.

I realized I had forgotten about my mom.

I turned to find my mom, waiting for news but already shattered to pieces. Her heart was broken completely when she heard my father had died. We cried together until she finally asked me to call her brother. Before long, everyone knew what had happened and plenty of help was on the way.

At home, neighbors waited for us, family gathered, and kids were back from school. The celery stew that my mom was preparing for lunch was still on the stove and the smell of celery had filled our small home. I remembered we hadn't eaten for hours.

Mom cried nonstop and neighbors comforted her. My younger sisters and brothers found a corner to cry. The sound of the Quran echoed through the whole house. Mourning and sobbing came from each corner, and my mom was louder than all.

She sobbed so loudly as she started losing her voice. I sat in the hallway on top of the stairs awake and numb; not knowing how to handle this horrible situation.

As I sat there, trying to figure out what would come next, I looked up and saw my father before me. At first, I was excited. I thought maybe he wasn't dead! He wasn't even sick. He looked younger, healthy, and happy. The figure of my father walked toward me, then stopped to point at my mom. He asked, "What is the matter with her? Why is she crying this much?"

I froze, thinking to myself, *"Because you're dead!"* I didn't need to say it out loud. It was as though he could hear my thoughts. He replied, "Tell her not to cry like this." Then he disappeared. I had no idea what had just happened. I was in shock. I knew I was awake; I knew I'd just seen him dead in the emergency room, but there he was in our house.

I finally realized that even though I didn't understand what had just happened, my father had sent me a message. From that point on, I was responsible for taking care of my mom. I had to make sure she was safe and sound.

On the third day after his passing, we had to have the memorial. The house was not empty. All aunts and uncles from different cities gathered there. With each new family member arriving, the crying and mourning got louder and louder. We recited the Quran and the sounds of it filled the house.

My dad's sister and my eldest sister and her family came all the way from *Mashad*. We hugged and cried over and over. The rest of the family and neighbors were working relentlessly to get the lunch ready for the memorial.

One of the neighbors came to me and kindly asked how I was doing?

"My back is broken." That was the first thing came out of my mouth and I thought to myself that I was only 23 but I felt old and aged; very old indeed.

Years later, I now see that life is very unpredictable; we don't know what's waiting for us. Even though at the time I felt great pain, it was a necessary pain. Pain is a tool to help us grow. After facing darkness and loss, we come out of it more mature and stronger.

Life after the death of my father was not the same. I started to become more responsible and caring, especially for my mom and my siblings.

Despite of all my challenges and all his disagreements, while he was sick, I was beside him and tried to help not only as his daughter but as an educated nurse. I could see a mixed feeling of admiration and regret in his eyes. I remembered my high school, university, radio contest, all I had done to have his attention; all that was not forgotten, but the acclamation which I could see in his eyes was enough to prove to me that I had chosen the right path.

Chapter 4: My Love Story, From Dating to Marriage

I had met some boys since starting university, but in an Islamic country, it was not easy to date. You were not allowed to see boys or hold hands in public. They might just come and jail you, or based on Sharia law, if you had kissed or touched a man who was not from your family (father, brother, or husband), they would fine you financially, emotionally, or even physically.

I saw how my classmates would meet boys at their places and how they talked about being kissed, making love, and sometimes only watching a movie together. I did not like that I couldn't go to boys' homes. I was afraid, and I didn't feel secure. All I did was walk with my boyfriend in parks and talk about different topics. In my last year at university, I met my husband. His mom had a heart attack, and I was doing my first shift in a private hospital. It was my last semester, and I had to get ready for my final exams.

I saw him while leaning against the hospital unit's radiator, deep in thought, staring into the distance. I looked at him and thought right away that I liked this guy.

He slowly came to my desk, looking kindly with a sparkle of mischief in his eyes.

"Would you like to work in a better hospital?" he asked, smiling warmly.

"I'm new and would like to make a lot of positive changes here," I responded with my head down, pretending to be busy by shuffling my patient's charts.

My heartbeats were fast, and my palms were sweaty, but I tried to play it cool. I tried to look at him without allowing him to see my interest in my eyes.

He didn't give up. "But my sister is a nurse in a very well-known hospital, if you ever consider…"

I was young and ambitious, with big dreams. I had come to this small, private hospital and I didn't agree with the system there and dreamed of changing the system.

"I want to make changes, and they need me here." That was my final answer.

Being a naive, unexperienced nurse student, I was lucky to have that job in CCU (Coronary Care Unit).

One day, he came to visit his mom, who had a heart attack and was hospitalized in our ward. I sat at the nursing station facing the elevator. He said goodbye and hit the elevator's button. When it was time to get in, he changed his mind, came back toward the water dispenser, and drank some water. I was watching him subtly. He went back again toward the elevator and turned his head toward the nursing station one more time. I knew he wanted to say something, but he was either shy or unsure.

"Take your heart with you!" I said with a teasing voice and smiled. He responded: "Pardon me?" I repeated loud and coy, "I said, take your heart with you." He finally left.

On my next shift, he came to my desk to ask if I would like to learn English.

"I have already been taking English classes at Meli's Institute," I replied. Meli's was one of the best in the country, but he offered me the chance to attend to the better one, which I couldn't refuse. We set a time and place so I could go and get the registration letter from him. And that was how we started seeing each other.

We dated each other outside a few times. We seemed to like each other, and both wanted to meet more often. In my heart, I chose him as my future husband. I told him that considering all existing dating limitations in our country, I did not want any hassle. My mom would not appreciate if I got arrested only because I was walking with a boy in public. All dating those days was done secretly, in such a fearful environment. I tried to stay away from being arrested or creating troubles and dishonour for my family.

At the end of my shifts, I knew he waited for me outside the hospital, well-groomed and anxious. My workplace was in a busy area of Tehran, very close to the *Vali-Asar* intersection where there was a busy and lively street full of parks, restaurants, cafes, and tea houses. We walked aimlessly on the streets around the hospital and sometimes would grab a juice or pizza in one of the places close by. We talked about everything and nothing, sometimes secretly holding hands despite the fear of getting arrested. But the excitement and feelings of being loved and loving my partner at such a young age helped me overcome the fear. We would even risk going inside a restaurant to eat together. Sitting beside him in a taxi when it was late, and he had to be with me until I was home safe and sound, was the warmest and most beautiful feeling a young girl could experience.

I wanted to marry him, since he had rubbed my heart and I had feelings for him but saying that and asking him to marry me was just not right. I finally told him about my family situation and that I was not planning to be only his girlfriend but his wife. I was 24 years old, almost finished with school, and wanted to look at my relationship with him more seriously. And I said to myself: *"If he was not ready to marry, we should stop seeing each other because I didn't want to waste my time by only dating."*

After a couple of months of dating, he came to my mom to ask for her permission to marry me. My mom trusted me 100%, but since my dad was not in the picture anymore, our distant family thought they had the right to interfere my decisions. They disagreed because they were against any marriage other than an arranged marriage. They tried so hard to convince me to change my mind, but I had made my mind up already and I decided to marry him no matter what.

We made plans for a formal marriage proposal. He came with his mom and uncle since he had also lost his dad. My mom had invited my cousin and her husband for the ceremony, too. The evening was tense because of a disagreement about my dowry. He and I had decided on every detail of the ceremony, and I didn't think my family would disagree with me.

We talked a lot and made plans for our future. We liked each other and had chemistry. He was always well-groomed and well-behaved. Like me, he studied at university and worked. He had a successful career and was a kind and loving man. I didn't find any reason to prevent me from marrying him. I even stood up against my family and my mom about my dowry. We decided to start with the least dowry in cash and not in gold, which was part of the marriage tradition back then. I did not believe in it. If a marriage does not work, who cares about a dowry? That was my philosophy. I should just leave both marriage and dowry if I'm not happy.

Regardless of all disagreements and threats from other close and distant family, I married him after three months of dating each other. We threw a small engagement party at his parent's house and announced our wedlock that day. Everyone was expecting a huge wedding in a big garden or something similar, but we decided to save this money for our own future. We were in such a great agreement in life that helped us grow and stay together in health and weakness.

Chapter 5: My Mother and Her Big Surprise

I felt so proud, pretending to be a serious teacher, dictating to my mom. To me, she was a slow writer, and it bored me. I was only in grade five. Mom never got a chance to go to school. All she had learned in her village was how to read the Quran.

She had five girls who could read and write, but she couldn't help them in their studies. She was determined to go to school, regardless.

There was an adult night school close to our home, and she went in the evenings. She was a very hard-working student. When she read, though, she read loud and slow. She repeated words to get the right pronunciation.

We kids helped her to get prepared for her exams. She was not very good at math, but her teacher encouraged her, and she loved the fact that she was able to write and read.

After finishing night school, she bought the newspaper and was busy half a day reading it loud and slow. We loved the fact that she was happy and satisfied. She read all the pages related to accidents, death, and bad news. There was one page in every newspaper called *Havades*, which means "Bad events." After reading this page, she'd always remind us to be cautious at school, carefully crossing the street, and to always be alert.

When my parents got married, they were complete strangers. They'd never met until the day of their wedding. My mom was young – only 19 years old.

They soon moved to Tehran from the village. Coming to a busy and chaotic city had been a big challenge for a young and simple girl like her. Dad rented a room in a big house that had a shared kitchen and bathroom. There were large rooms that each housed one family. My parents had to wash the dishes and clothes in the big backyard.

They got pregnant and had their babies in that house with the help of a traditional midwife. Life wasn't easy but they were happy regardless of all challenges.

After a while, they moved out and got a house in the centre of town. I was born there. On the second day after my birth, my mom fell asleep while breastfeeding me. When she woke up and checked on me to see if I needed to be changed, she saw blood all over my Band-Aid. The midwife didn't care much to cut my umbilical cord properly, and I had bled to the point that my mom said I looked like a ghost. They somehow managed to stop the bleeding, but all the midwife cared to do was to wash my bands quickly to try to hide any evidence so I wouldn't have to go to hospital or to avoid my dad reporting to her.

Mom was unique. She never lied or harmed anyone. She was so powerful and resilient. Although she was from a village, she was very open-minded and minded of her own business. All winter, she knitted jackets, gloves, or hats for us. She sat beside our oil heater with a kettle and a teapot on it and knitted. At the same time, she managed the house and watched us. I still cannot imagine how she could handle 11 pregnancies and raising nine children. When Dad died, she was still young and had men interested in marrying her, but she decided to be a single mom and raise us well.

Dad was gone and we were a big family. Mom was young and had been very dependent on our dad. Since dad was the decision maker in the centre of our family, Mom never learned how to make big decisions or handle difficult situations.

Give a woman the opportunity, she will change your world for the better. Give her wings, she will fly above and beyond. Mom had learned how to read the Quran in the correct way from our dad. She translated the verses in Farsi and analyzed the meaning of each section. She learnt from Dad about Islam's history and all the events that happened in Prophet Mohammad's life.

One thing that is for certain, however; never underestimate the power of a woman. Up until now, I don't know how she was able to gather herself after Dad's death in a powerful way. She had changed significantly and wasn't the same woman as before: obedient, indecisive, and passive. I don't know how she managed to get a lot of women involved as her students, but she became a Quran teacher and started running classes for young and middle-aged women. She had more than 10 students and was paid for classes. Our home became like a classroom and every morning from 9:00 a.m. to 12:00 p.m., there was a class. This gave her more and more confidence and she started to look like a powerful woman in our family and neighborhood.

As Rumi says, "The wound is the place where the light enters you." The light of love can only reach our hearts through the cracks created by the darkness. It's clear that we grow from our pain. Despite all intended interruptions from male power on her side of the family, she learnt to speak up for herself and her kids. She didn't tolerate any insults or abusive behaviours. There was a married man interested in marrying my mom as well, and he came to ask her for an Islamic temporary marriage, which is called *Seighae.*

"I won't exchange one hair of my children for hundreds of you," she told him.

Everyone was worried about her. They wondered how she would be able to raise all these kids. Could she to send them to school, get the girls' dowries, and provide the boys' wedding ceremonies?

These were everyone's concerns, but Mom wouldn't take pity and was certain of her ability to raise us well and proud.

It was almost the time for my wedding and my mom asked me to go with her to our backroom. There was a closet there where we kept our clothes. She searched behind her own pack of clothes and handed me a bag full of money!

My eyes widened in surprise, and I said, "What is this?"

She said, "This is all the money you've been giving me since your dad passed away to spend at home. I didn't touch it."

How stupid was I? For almost two years, I thought I was the one who brought bread to the house! I worked in two hospitals at the same time; I was a full-time student at nursing university trying to feed my mom and my siblings. She never told us about the savings she had and how hard she'd worked to get my dad's salary. She won over paperwork and a corrupted system without getting help from anyone. Being a widow and having all those young kids was a big challenge on its own, let alone feeding them, sending them to school, and making sure they were raised properly and would continue their education at high levels. I still wonder how she wasn't completely broken.

Moms are unique. A human being as a mom is a blessing with millions of unspoken feelings that you wouldn't want to exchange for the whole world. All mothers' desires are summarized in one wish: the best for their children. No matter how they are suffering, they are still accommodating their family's needs instead of theirs.

We face challenges and we have no idea how strong we can be and how resilient we are. Women — especially Middle Eastern women — are so resilient and powerful. They face abusive relationships, humiliations, and loneliness, yet they grow like flowers from the dirt that has been thrown at them. They transform into beautiful butterflies from silkworm trapped in men's world and men's power.

Chapter 6: I Became a Mother

It was almost mid-February 1994 - the evening before Valentine's Day. I had abdominal cramps. I was nearly nine months pregnant, but not due yet. Another 21 days remained before the baby was ready, as my doctor said. It was snowing hard outside like there was no boundary between ground and sky. It was pure white everywhere, as though I saw a blank page with no lines. Soon, I would flip another page of my life and start a brand-new chapter in motherhood.

I knew I shouldn't have this bleeding, this cramping. It was too early for the baby, and I was worried that something was wrong. This new chapter of my life was supposed to be white and pure, but these bloody spots made me so anxious; I could barely breathe.

We didn't have a car, or even a home phone, and had to make calls from our neighbor's home. My husband called the doctor, and they told us to come for an immediate checkup. The doctor triaged me and said, "It's almost time; you can come back to the hospital around midnight." It was almost 4:00 p.m.

We decided to do some shopping to help the labour along, and then go back home. We went out to buy groceries: meats, fruits, and vegetables so we could prepare for this new family member. We came back home and started packing; then we started cutting the meat to put it in the freezer.

My husband asked his mom for help. She was lovely, so caring, and very excited about the birth of her first grandchild from her eldest child. She recalled an old tale she had been told and suggested that I drink Coke to help have an easy labour. It sounded strange, but I listened to her. The cramp pains came and went. At nearly 10:00 p.m., the contractions were so bad that I couldn't even eat dinner. I decided I would go take a shower and do whatever I needed to prepare myself for staying in the hospital. I probably wouldn't have time to take care of myself properly for a while. I cut my nails and thoroughly cleaned myself.

Around midnight, the pain was so intense I couldn't take it anymore. I asked my husband to call the taxi; we needed to go to hospital right away. We bundled up in our winter coats with hats and gloves. Despite my discomfort, it was a magical night. The snow reflected the moonlight in a beautiful glow as I stepped into the yard, it reached my knees.

I took a deep breath and tried to sense motherhood with every cell in my body. I was about to become a mother. How strange was this feeling? It was an amalgamation of excitement, love, and fear. My mother-in-law came with us, and that gave me a bit of relief. She knew what was coming for me.

We went to a hospital in the north of Tehran, one of the best private hospitals in town. My gynecologist was known as a doctor with golden hands. He was also a surgeon. We arrived, and I introduced myself to labour and delivery. There were no patients, only me. The midwives talked and laughed so loud. When they saw me, they didn't seem happy. I knew - I worked in a hospital myself. At midnight, you wanted to have a good quiet night, but now there was a patient. I was certain they were not happy. I was in a lot of pain but tried to be nice.

One of them came and asked me to go and lie down on the bed so she could examine me. My contractions were so bad that I couldn't even think straight. I put my head on the wrong side, and she got so upset. She gruffly said, "Head here, tail there."

I was so offended and heartbroken. How dare she talk to a patient in a private hospital like that? After all, we were paying for this night. I didn't see any respect, but I apologized and changed my position. She examined me. It was so painful. I cried; I screamed.

In 1994, our families were not allowed to come to the labour and delivery room. New mothers were all by themselves. My husband and his mom waited outside. No man could stay with a patient in the delivery room. He didn't feel the anguish with me, and he couldn't hold my hand to soothe me while I was in pain. I was alone with that nasty midwife.

She examined me at 5:00 a.m. and said, "It's too early to have you push."

"But my pain is bad," I told her.

"You have to stay patient. It isn't time yet," she replied.

It was a long and excruciating night. From midnight until nine in the morning, I had to bear the pain. I was in labour, screaming and sweating, and my husband and his mom couldn't come inside; the rules wouldn't let them. My doctor was not there either, because I was not ready to deliver this baby yet.

Around six in the morning, the midwife checked my progress again.

"I can see the baby's head," she exclaimed as she ran to call the doctor.

The doctor was at home in the shower.

I didn't know what to do. I felt that I needed to go to the bathroom. "Please, may I use the bathroom?" I asked.

The midwife let me, even though she could see the baby's head and this urge was the labour, not a need for the toilet.

She said again that she could see the baby's head. I couldn't even think straight. I needed to pee. I got to the bathroom, and before I reached the toilet, a gush of liquid hit the floor: my water broke.

I came back into the room, and she checked my cervix again.

"Your water just broke! That wasn't the head of your baby!" she said.

Stupid her. She called the doctor and said she made a mistake, so now the doctor was not in a rush. He came around 8:00 a.m. and examined me.

"I can't take it anymore," I said, exhausted and at my wits' end.

He told his assistant, "Let's get the operating room ready. We are going to do a C-section."

I complained. "After nine hours of pain and contractions, now you're taking me to the operating room. So why did I suffer this much? Why did my baby suffer?"

I cried nonstop, and I said, "I am going to deliver naturally."

He said, "I'll give you one more chance, and you push."

I was so exhausted, but I didn't want to go to the operating room after nine hours of being in labour. I tried my best; I screamed and pushed. I kept calling my husband's name, but I didn't hear anything from him. They said it looked like he was gone home. I was so mad. I didn't know what happened; maybe he waited too long, perhaps he got tired, maybe they told him to go home.

My baby came at 9:05 a.m. on Valentine's Day: February 14, 1994. He was so tiny that I was scared to hug him. I didn't understand why, but back then, they didn't put the baby on the mother's chest. They just grabbed the baby from me, cleaned him, and put him in the incubator. My head was spinning. I looked at my baby; I smiled. I was in awe of how happy I felt. That was one shiny corner of happiness.

The doctor started putting some stitches in me. He needed to make another cut to put the stitches in properly. I couldn't believe the pain. My head spun: I was so pale, and my mouth was so dry. They carried me to the ward.

They called my husband's name but got no answer. Where was my family?

Nobody was waiting for me in the hallway. I kept turning my head, checking around every corner to see if there was somebody here. There was no one. They took me to the recovery room, and I broke down and burst into tears. I didn't know how long it was before my husband finally came. He brought me a deodorant spray as a gift for my son's delivery. This gift surprised me. I was expecting a big gold chain or something precious or expensive. Who would give such a cheap gift on his own son's birthday? He sent me a note many years after explaining that because we weren't supposed to have the baby that soon, he wasn't prepared to get me a proper gift. At that moment, and even after so many years, I was too tired to discuss it with him. I tried to focus on the positive side. I was a mother of a healthy boy, and he was his dad; nothing else mattered.

There are an unlimited number of lessons mothers learn. Perspectives change a lot. Pregnancies and labour could be the most painful experiences a human being could experience, but I will not exchange it for anything else. The feelings of having a child of your own are the most rewarding feelings.

By becoming a parent, one will be changed mentally, emotionally, and spiritually; another one may be transformed into a selfless, loving, and proud person. Everything in life will lose the importance and only one concern highlights your existence: your child's well-being.

We learn to stay up all night with no regret, we learn to sacrifice, we learn to be selfless, and all attentions move from our ego to something bigger and broader. It's not that we help our child to grow, we grow through them, and we find a part inside ourselves that we never thought it existed.

Chapter 7: Something Unexpected Shattered My Heart, My Sister, Atefeh

The impact of some life events and traumas are so deep. They can crush us emotionally and physically and transform us into a brand-new person. We wish we could prevent loss, accident, or disease, but sometimes they happen to change our life trajectory or complete our mission in this life.

Recently, one of my sisters shared our sister Atefeh's handwriting, remembering her on the anniversary of her death.

Atefeh means affection and heart and exactly represents the way she was. Kind, affectionate, and considerate. My sister placed Atefeh's handwriting on her door - a poem. When we don't have the power to change our surroundings or other people's attitude toward us, we have no option but to accept them the way they are and accept our destiny.

Atefeh was a beautiful, tall, and smart girl. She was the fifth girl in our family and very different from all her other siblings. She dreamed of continuing her studies in Japan or Germany and traveling the world. She was very ambitious. The next sibling born after her was the first-born son. He got all the attention from my parents, especially my dad. The age gap between them was not much. I recall their childhood, playing and fighting together. Atefeh had a big heart and was full of energy and aspiration. To me, she didn't belong to her place and time. She was ahead of her friends. She was a forward thinker who believed differently, loved passionately, and cared unlimitedly.

When she was in high school, she fell in love with a boy in our neighborhood. The boy was from a very low-class family with no integrity. None of us liked him. He was a jerk, but he was able to steal Atefeh's innocent heart. We all asked her to forget him, and we all blamed her for choosing this type of guy. Instead, she decided to hide her ongoing relationship with him.

One morning I was on the bus on my way to university, and we drove past a big park in our neighborhood. It was a gloomy morning. The bus was busy, and I stood, looking from dirty windows to the crowd, watching people's commutes on the crowded streets of Tehran. The bus passed the park, and, through the window, I saw the guy with my sister, walking hand in hand in the park. I was furious, thinking she should be at school by now. I knew the guy had dropped out of school because he was a lazy jerk. I thought to myself, "*He's being a yank taking my sister to the park when she should be at school.*" I knew I would be late for my own class if I got off the bus, but I decided to do so. At the next stop, I got off the jam-packed bus and moved back toward the park. I was mad, walking on the sidewalk and thinking about what to tell them.

I finally found them and called out to my sister. She turned her head back and he paused. They both were so scared when they saw me; they were like kids getting caught while doing something bad. I blamed her for allowing him to steal her dreams. Something inside told me this would ruin her life and prevent her from following her dreams of higher education and immigrating abroad. I questioned her if our late dad would be happy witnessing this kind of behaviour from his daughter?

They were both silent. They just shamefully stared at me and listened. There was nothing to defend, nothing to hide or justify. After a few minutes of silence, she slowly said, "I love him, and I would do anything to be with him."

I was speechless! What could I tell her? How could I show her the guy she fell in love with was not the right person for her? How could I convince her to leave him and remember her dreams? Love blinded her. She couldn't think straight, and she thought all her dreams might exist in him.

I told her, "You deserve better than him. What does he have? Good education? Good job? Good family? Living with him will make you miserable. You are smart, beautiful, and dedicated. You deserve way better."

But it was too late. I couldn't open her eyes; I didn't know how to help her.

I left them in the park, so mad and so disappointed. All our family, even that jerk's family, were against their relationship. Atefeh convinced her boyfriend to marry her since she thought they couldn't continue this relationship in secret.

One night, I was asked to visit my mom and attend a family gathering for the traditional proposal ceremony. Atefeh cleaned the house and prepared the fruits and tea. Her boyfriend didn't come with his parents, or any member of his family except a girl and a boy he introduced as his cousins. Later, we found out they were only distant friends to him. But Atefeh didn't care. She was determined to marry him. She was a child who didn't know better. Although that marriage shouldn't have happened, none of us could have prevented it. That portentous marriage was part of their destiny.

She was very young in her late teens, and he was just a couple of years older than her. A few weeks later, they threw a wedding party with a small group of people. We went into a very small family group, and we were not excited to dress up nicely. We were heartbroken and bitter; all of us had stored anger and dissatisfaction in our hearts. I wanted to scream and end all this stupid ceremony, but I couldn't move. She smiled and looked happy and unaware of her bad fortune.

The wedding was simple and quiet. There was no dancing, no happy cheers. At least, I don't recall any happy memories.

We didn't do any of the traditional ceremonies for the bride and groom. We didn't invite them to our houses for *Pagosha* (the welcoming ceremony for bride and groom). We didn't greet the groom as our family member. His family did the same. They didn't welcome Atefeh as their bride. His mom and sisters were so mean and unfair to this young, beautiful bride. And since then, she started a lonely life in an unwelcoming family with no respect or value. She made her choice at the age of 19 and stepped into hell.

Months later, on a warm September evening, my neighbor, who was an old, kind, and warm lady, called me from our backyard and told me we had a phone call. We didn't have any landline or mobile at that time. My son was only two years old, and my husband was in his tutoring class. I rushed there, and I heard my mom's neighbor's voice trying to be calm but shivering, telling me something bad had happened and I should rush to my mom's house.

Immediately I was worried about my mom, asking if something had happened to her? She said, "Your mom is okay!"

I was relieved and thought, *"Nothing's wrong then."* I called my husband's friend because my husband was at their place tutoring their son. We didn't have a car. My husband came with his friend to pick me up.

In greater Tehran, it was hard to travel, and traffic was heavy. We lived in the north of Tehran, and Mom lived in the west, while this friend lived on the east side. It took forever. I marched up and down in our condominium until they arrived, not knowing what was expected of me. I wasn't sure if I needed to pack my clothes, or how long I would be at my mom's. I took my two-year-old son and jumped into the car. I suspected they knew what was happening, but they didn't know how to tell me. I told them I was not worried since I knew my mom was fine, but my hands were cold, and my legs were shaking. There was a butterfly in my stomach wandering and flying desperately. My bladder was about to explode under stress, and as soon as we reached my mom's house, I rushed into the bathroom in the backyard but was unable to collect myself.

I was overwhelmed with so many questions and a strange feeling. I wondered what was happening and couldn't wait to get out and satisfy my curiosity. I walked into the hallway. My brother, who was only a teenager at the time, sat on the stairs holding his head in his hands.

I asked, "How's Mom? Where is she?"

He said, "Nobody is home. They're all gone to Atefeh's house."

She lived with her in-laws just two alleys from Mom. I left my son with his uncle and rushed there. All the neighbours and families were outside her house, circling and whispering. It was dark, and I didn't even ask what had happened. I immediately knew something bad had happened to Atefeh.

I heard the whispers: "Did he hang her?" "Where is he now?" "Where are his mom and sister?"

One of her neighbors, who lived downstairs as their tenant, was mumbling while crying. She said, "He was hitting her every single night and I could hear her crying, begging him to stop hitting her and reminding him to love her. I could hear he was banging her head to the walls, and she was screaming from pain. I couldn't do anything because his mom was supporting him and encouraging him to do so and to be crueler to her since she didn't like her."

I couldn't believe that much savage cruelty. How could a human being be that brutal to a young, innocent girl?

I couldn't even cry. My eyes were dry, and tears would not fall. I was in bitter shock and disbelief. My husband held my hand tight. I started talking loudly, thinking they were inside of the house hiding and they could hear me.

I said, "She was so innocent. She was gorgeous with big eyes, with a warm and kind heart, with big dreams. Was this the heaven you promised her? Where are you to come and face me and tell me that you have broken your promises? You told us you were going to make her a queen. You said you loved her. You are a liar. She loved you, and despite all odds, she chose you. You made a grave for her in her dream nest."

I was loud and furious. I wasn't even crying. I went on and on, and everyone in that circle was sobbing and crying.

I exclaimed, "Why are you all hiding like mice?"

My mom was sobbing, saying her young daughter came to her a few days before telling her she had a dream. In her dream, she was complaining to our dad about her husband, that he's so cruel to her, and Dad told her come to me, pointing at his side, telling her, "Come and lie down beside me."

We buried her very close to our dad in the cemetery. It was very strange that the computer in the cemetery chose her grave so close to our dad, even though it had been years since we buried him in that sector. We were shocked, knowing she would be only steps away from our dad's grave.

We never saw her cruel husband afterward. When I remember reading the coroner's report and criminal police report with my wet eyes, there were old hematomas in different areas on her head indicating she'd been hit with a hard object; a trace of a hard object was found on her neck, and signs of suffocation from hanging for a long time. There were numerous bruises and scratches on her body. They forgot to write "and a broken heart!"

We were too heartbroken to follow her husband or take it to court. My sister was gone, and nothing could bring her back.

She was abandoned since my first brother was born. Our father left us when she was little. The fear of loss and abandonment made her fill the gap by finding love and living with someone she thought loved her. When she married out of the blue, despite all their disagreements, she was left alone again. We didn't know she was beaten. We were not aware of how they behaved and how she handled her situation. Simply, we were too angry and disappointed to interfere. We might just think, "*Let her live her own life,*" and she didn't dare to come and talk to us. I regret that I didn't visit her, was not closer to her, and I didn't give her space to open her heart and ask for help. The trauma deeply affected our family but made us kinder, more considerate, and much closer. Even if any of us wanted to follow his/her own way, we have never left each other. Atefeh opened our hearts as her name represents: she taught us how to be more affectionate and caring toward whom we love, especially our family.

If your family member has abandoned you, please watch them from a distance and see what they are doing and with whom they deal. Find an expert consultant and try to find a way to enter their life again. Don't leave them alone until it's too late. They may really need someone to talk to and they don't dare to get back to you again.

Chapter 8: Are We Moving to A Dreamland?

Living with my husband was good and pleasant for several years. We made plans together for our future life and everyone envied us. In less than a year, we got our own condominium. We decided to sell all our furniture and cash in all our gold and gifts from our wedding to buy a house.

Everyone told us we were wrong, but we proved them wrong instead. We could go to the moon together. We could do anything, anything that seemed impossible to others. For close to a year, we lived in an almost empty apartment with no stove, no TV, no furniture, because we spent everything on buying that apartment. We worked hard together and with every paycheck, we would buy one necessary piece of furniture. A year later, we had almost everything.

Marriage is not all about roses and hugs. A true marriage is about seeing your partner at their worst and still loving them and wiping their tears while they are crying. Having your shoulders for them when they need to lean on you.

Marriage can be ugly. You see the absolute worst in your partner when they are sad, mad, down, and blue. Women are in pain while menstruating; you hear your man snoring and that may not let you sleep; they empty their stomach's gas in sleep and your nose cannot take the smell. You smell the bad breath when you want to kiss them. Good marriage isn't all roses and romantic dinners, but it is amazing when you still talk to each other while your heads are on one pillow until morning. When you wake up with a gentle kiss on your shoulders. When you fight over simple and stupid matters and with one kind and warm look, all ugly discussions are forgotten. A good marriage can be beautiful at the same time. When you come back from work exhausted and impatient, they rub your feet and your back, and you can relax and ease your tough day. It's a mishmash of everything put into one.

He was a hard worker, starting early in the morning and coming home late at night. One night, he came home and as soon as I heard him coming, I rushed to the door. I opened the door with a big smile on my face. I hugged him and smothered him with kisses; then I showed him my tummy and said, "Hello, Daddy." He couldn't believe it. He excitingly hugged me, kissed me and my tummy, and said hello to our little baby. I worked in the hospital my whole pregnancy. The last month of my pregnancy was really hard; it was winter, and I was getting heavier. The nursing job wasn't getting easier at all. I dragged myself to the end of the pregnancy. There were nights I couldn't lie down and sleep. I had to sit up to sleep. I had a lot of shortness of breath as soon as I'd lie down.

When We Left Our Homeland

By the time our son was born, we were settled properly. I remember our neighbor's daughter called us "a perfect family."

Life was good for the three of us. We had almost everything. Young people looked at us like their role models and older ones admired us.

This perfect family decided to migrate to Canada when our son started going to elementary school. There, we noticed he was not receiving a proper education. Our son was super intelligent and Islamic schools were poisoning his mind with religious material, which we did not believe in.

I remember taking our son for an IQ test when he was only five. The psychology instructor congratulated us for having an intelligent, unique child. I burst into tears after hearing that.

Seemingly surprised, she asked, "Why are you crying? You should be happy!"

I said, "No, having this kind of gift, give us a great responsibility and I'm not sure if I'm capable enough to raise him as he deserves. He needs more intelligent parenting and I'm afraid if we don't have that."

Since then, we listened to our coach, and I took sessions with a well-known psychologist to learn how to raise my child the way he deserved. I read a lot of books regarding the right way to raise our child. I tried hard to do the best for him. His dad, on the other hand, was super busy working 12 hours per day to make a living for us. I didn't go back to work after my three-month maternity leave, since I knew raising a human being was the most difficult job I had. When our son was five and a half years old, I returned to work in a hospital very close to our home.

His dad and I tried our best to send him to the best daycares, music classes, swimming lessons, etc. He was the only child and we both loved him so dearly.

Our family had almost everything back then: a nice apartment in the best neighbourhood, a nice car, great careers and high income. But one thing, one big thing, was missing. We were not certain about our family's future. My husband had wanted to leave the country for a better life while he was single, he even tried it before, but he could not succeed. He planned to try again.

We applied to immigrate to Canada, filing all the paperwork on our own and without an attorney. We waited anxiously for word but were not approved for the first time. Back then, there was no high-speed Internet and even the telephone system wasn't very good. It was hard to get everything translated and stamped with the proper credentials. My English wasn't very good and so my husband had to do everything. Even though he was successful in his career and made a good income,

Canadian immigration denied our paperwork because it wasn't filled out right. We were sad, but not ready to give up.

One late afternoon, I had an appointment with a famous immigration lawyer at Yousef-Abad Street. I took a taxi there and made sure I put on my nicest clothes. I bought a beautiful flower basket and went to see this famous and expensive lawyer. Coming back home, I was anxious to give the news to my husband: the lawyer was very optimistic he could get us to Canada.

We were ready to spend as much as money we needed in order to be able to leave the country, but we wanted everything to be legal. We applied as legal immigrants and were told that we only need to wait for two to three years. Three years seemed like a long way to go, but no other options were available. In the meantime, I worked on my English proficiency with the help of my husband since he was fluent. He sent me to the best English school in town. I started taking piano lessons and when we got a car, I was happily driving in the city. I went to the gym regularly, took dance classes, went to different workshops, and got ready to start a new life in Canada. We also sent our son to one of the best English institutes through my husband's connections.

Then, September 11, 2001, happened in New York and all immigration files were put on hold. We had to wait another two years! We were furious and mad, but still patient and hopeful.

Our interview at the Canadian embassy was held in Rome, Italy. It was late February and the week of our son's birthday. We flew there. We could not take our son since they gave visas only to two people: my husband and I. We stayed one week in Italy. I cried all the time since I missed my son. It was the first time I left him for a long-distance trip. It was 2002, the cell phones and Internet were still very slow, and it was hard to use them to communicate. We had to go to public phone kiosks and use a loaded card to make long-distance calls. The reception was bad, and I could not talk to my son who was at home with his aunty. I cried every night, missing him, and did not enjoy Italy at all.

The interview went very well since my husband spoke like a native Canadian and impressed the Canadian officer so much. We knew we had passed the interview, but we were still anxious about any kind of surprises. We came back home with lots of toys and gifts for our son.

Spring arrived with hope and warmth. Our condominium had a huge, beautiful yard with beds of flowers and shrubs in it. In *Shemiran* (north of Tehran), there used to be big gardens. Our place was one of the ones they had changed into a three-story condominium, but they kept a part of the garden in a yard with a tall walnut tree in it. The previous owners were a kind old couple who were our neighbors. They took care of the flowers, trees, and greenery with their big heart and kind soul all the time. We didn't miss being far from our families. They were like grandparents to our son and loved him dearly. Our son learnt how to bike in that vast yard with his dad's help. He played soccer with the neighbor's kids there. We all enjoyed the beautiful and green *Shemiran*, with good weather and cooler summer than Tehran. *Shemiran* was part of Greater Tehran, but in the north and very close to the Alborz Mountains. Every Friday, our family arranged a picnic or mountain climbing with two of our other family friends who were my husband's colleagues that had girls close to our son's age. Even now, these kids stay in touch and are still close to each other. We enjoyed getting together occasionally and throwing birthday parties for our kids.

Enjoying being in nature and protecting the mountains and green fields was one of the lessons we taught our children. They climbed the mountains alongside us with those small feet and big smiles on their faces. They loved to be part of our adventures. Our son was so happy growing in such a lovely environment.

Did we want another kid? Yes, but since we wanted to migrate soon, every plan was postponed until we got to the land of our dreams. We then planned to have another child. We never thought it would take such a long time that by the time we settled in the land of dreams, our son would be a teenager and we would ignore the idea of having another child.

One beautiful day the mail came with great news in it… we were accepted and had passed the interview. I danced with the mail in my hand and kissed my son over and over. He jumped up and down, seeing my happiness and celebrated with me. I kept repeating to him, "We are going to Canada. We are going to Canada…" My innocent baby didn't understand what I meant. He was just as happy as me and continued dancing with me. My husband came home late in the evening, and we celebrated again.

Our next step was to run our medical exams and finally in 2004 we got our visas… yay! After five years of fighting for this, we could go to Canada: the land of everyone's dream and opportunity!

Our families were happy for us, and at the same time it was a bittersweet feeling. My aunt (my youngest aunt from my mom's side) tried hard to convince me I should not do this for the sake of my old mom. She said I should stay and hang around since she might need my help. My mom, on the other hand, wanted the best for me, and as always, prayed nonstop for our happiness and health and whatever made us happy.

It was June when we flew to Toronto, all three of us with our hearts full of hope and excitement. Our now 10-year-old son was super anxious, though polite and well-mannered. He ate his ham sandwich on the long flight and told me he did not like the taste. I tried to convince him that from now on there would be a lot of new experiences and we should adapt ourselves to changes. We might face stuff that we did not like, but we should adapt. My innocent child agreed and ate his ham sandwich anyway. I had a bite myself and I could not finish it. Back home, ham was not provided, and we were not familiar with the taste. I could not finish my sandwich, but I promised myself I would try my best to like everything in my new country.

We landed on a hot day in Toronto. Coming outside Pearson, we saw people smoking cigarettes. My son was surprised and a little disappointed, saying, "Oh! They smoke here too!!!" I guess we thought the land of dreams might look totally different, no smoking, no traffic, and no pollution. We expected to smell and taste the best!! We imagined a piece of heaven to be seen.

Soon we found out nowhere was perfect. Everywhere has its own rules and challenges. The van which our friend booked for us came to take us to an Iranian lodging that was well known at that time in Toronto. It was one of the few places for Iranians who knew nothing about Canada to stay when they first arrived.

We were so naive and uneducated about Canada and where we would stay. These people took a great advantage of us and other newcomers.

In the middle of the night, I felt claustrophobic; I could not breathe in this damp, small bedroom which held all three of us in it. I tried to escape outside. The ceiling was too low, and I could reach it with my short height. The room was too small to move around in. I was out of breath since there was no air conditioner. It was a hot, humid night and I thought $100 American for this hole was not really worth it. How were we going to survive here?

We stayed three nights in that damp room. My husband's friend finally came and rescued us. Staying at his flat was much better, but we could not bother him. No one would give us any rental place. We had no Canadian credits since we just arrived. We did not have enough time to build a credit. At last, we got to our lawyer's office in Toronto, and they got us to an old building to settle in. We paid the first and last month's rental fee and we temporarily settled there. Then we started buying furniture and in less than a month were almost out of our savings.

We needed to register for our courses, our exams, and driver's licenses, but everything required Canadian dollars. When we exchanged Iranian currency (Rial to Canadian dollar), there was not enough to pay for our expenses. All our savings over years back home were emptying so fast.

We used to have a comfortable life back home, and this building was old and smelly. We headed toward the elevator and noticed a man with a lot of big, heavy dogs getting on. We did not know how to react to being inside the elevator with these large dogs. This was another country, and we were not familiar with the rules. Maybe it was what it was. We were disappointed and sad, but we had to carry on.

I was afraid of answering phones. Even though I knew English, I could not understand all accents. While shopping, we faced different nationalities and accents and trying to understand them was killing my confidence. Gradually I stopped speaking English. My husband, on the other hand, managed the language part wonderfully and accompanied me everywhere, acting as my translator.

We went to nursing college, and he did all the talking and enrolled me for exams.

It was time to study hard. He worked as a security guard for night shifts and spent the days studying in college.

I studied with his help to equalize my nursing degree to Canada's degree. At the same time, I also studied English and took the exams accordingly. Our money was running out, though, and it was getting hard to continue.

Our son had his own challenges adapting to school, especially with his English. Life was definitely not turning out the way we planned. We walked on eggshells. Everything was so tense. After six months of fighting these battles, we sat in the kitchen, hand in hand, to discuss our future. We talked and cried together. We missed our life back home, our social status, our privileges, and our high standard of living. Here, we did not even have a car. We lived in an old rental building with cockroaches in the kitchen cabinets. We cried together and made a vow; we were going to give it another six-month trial. If things did not change, we would pack up and leave. We still had our home back in Iran. We could get our jobs back easily and we could at least say we tried.

When you plan meticulously and expect everything to go as planned, if things don't happen as you planned, trust the fact that there are reasons behind it and the universe has better plans for you. Don't fight with it and don't get disappointed.

In December that year, I passed my nursing exam. Life began to show us its beauty one more time.

Chapter 9: That Was Not What I Expected Either! My Separation Story

I woke up with my heart beating fast, cold sweat on my body, panting. I sat on the bed and turned my head toward him; he was in a deep sleep lying on his side of the bed. He was here. I took a deep breath and thought, "This is not the first time I have dreamed like this. Why do I have these nightmares?" Sometimes I dreamed I lost my shoes, or they were coming apart. I was barefoot, nervous, and anxious, looking for my shoes everywhere. I didn't know where I could find them. Why did I keep having these dreams? I tried to go back to sleep, but seeing this nightmare again scared me.

I had checked the interpretation of this kind of repetitive dreams before. I did not want to believe in them. Shoes in a dream mean relationship. Losing a pair of shoes means losing the partner, and having old, torn-up shoes means separation. I knew that, but I didn't want to tell anyone about my nightmares. I didn't even want to remind myself.

It had been 29 years since our wedding, and we had built a life together. Our marriage was not an arranged marriage; we married based on love. We immigrated to Canada and went through so many ups and downs together. We were so proud of what we built. Our life was not perfect. We had fights, challenges, and disagreements like any other marriage, but those seemed healthy to me. People told us we looked great as a couple. We had everything that a couple might wish for; a great home, good cars, high income, and an absolutely loving son who was one in a million. He was caring, kind-hearted, and loving. He was the perfect son every parent wishes for.

It was almost my husband's birthday, and I had already invited 60 people. Like nearly every year for the past three years, I ordered a three-layer cake. It was summer, and the right timing to throw a party in the backyard. This year, he put a great large gazebo in the backyard; it was beautiful, vast, and green. The flowerbeds were full of buds and flowers, and the stone-made patio looked gorgeous. Everything was ready, and I was excited to celebrate these happy moments with others. This gathering had become an annual ritual for us. I announced it to my family friends both locally and from other cities and asked them to mark their calendars. The party was only two weeks away when I found out the real meaning of my nightmares. Unfortunately, my sixth sense hadn't lied to me. I discovered photos and text messages of him dating different women, not only one, over the past few years. I realized I had fooled myself with lies for ages. I had brushed off the signs, his ignorance, our irrational fights, and his mood swings. My mind started putting together all the evidence to complete the puzzle. This was too overwhelming. "How can I put it up with all of this? No, I cannot deny the truth anymore," I said to myself.

I left home, saying nothing, while crying so hard. I couldn't breathe easily or think straight. I had a hard time sleeping at night as I wasn't eating properly for a month. I could not tell my family what was happening to me. It devastated me. My heart shattered into pieces. Nobody could imagine if I filed for divorce. To me, living a separate life was still unbelievable. I was in denial, in doubt, reviewing all the evidence that I tried to ignore for years. The wistful palace we built together, the dream I thought was real, finally collapsed. Nightmares came to reality, and everything made sense. All those doubts and all those questions were answered. When we cancelled the birthday party, everybody was in shock.

It is devastating, disgusting, and terrible to read all those sexy texts, and imagine that partner in bed making love with your husband while you were working the night shift in the hospital. No one deserves to face this crisis. But let me tell you: the first thing you need to do is to get counselling and a therapist for yourself, because believe me, this pain is not comparable to any other pain! It's so deep, so raw, and sharp!

I didn't tell my family back home. One day, I received many messages from my younger sister; she wanted to talk to me. I ignored her messages because I didn't want to talk about my situation with anyone. Finally, her daughter, my niece, reached out to me, mentioning that they were worried about me and would like to hear my voice.

I picked up the phone and said, "I'm fine. I am okay. What's wrong?"

"You are not okay. I know you're not," she replied.

I burst into tears and finally told her what had happened.

She cried with me and said, "While climbing the Alborz Mountains, on the Damavand's peak, I had a gut feeling. I saw your face crying so hard; the tears were rolling down from your eyes, and you were mumbling: 'He cheated on me! He devastated me.'"

She cried so hard that I had to comfort her.

"That was not fair to you. Cheating on you was the most unfair thing that could have happened to you. You have been so loyal; you have a big heart and kind soul. Cheating on anybody else could be somehow understandable, but not on you!" she said.

My brother called. I didn't know how to tell him. He might never understand me. I couldn't stop crying. My words became lost in my whimper. He didn't realize what I said.

"Take a deep breath and then talk," he said.

"I cannot breathe," I replied and then explained it all.

"My dearest sister, my love! How could he? Maybe you are wrong. It's a big mistake. This is not possible. He loved you, and you loved him. He loved his family. He was so dedicated to you. You both had the best life; you both were role models for everybody. We all wanted to be like you guys! This is not possible. You are delusional..." He couldn't understand what had happened.

We all agreed Mom should not know this under any circumstances. She should not be aware of what just happened. She had always felt so relieved that I had the best life on the other side of the world. She thought I was happy. She was so proud of me. Everybody agreed to that! We all promised to keep it a secret from her.

One week after the call with my brother, Mom called me. I tried to sound calm as usual; nothing had changed in my life. Everything was just fine, I pretended.

"I have bad feelings," she told me.

I asked, "What kind of feelings?" And I told her everything was okay.

"What's wrong? My instinct tells me something's wrong. My heart aches for you. I see you crying all the time, not in dreams, though! I see your face. You are upset, you are very sad!" she says.

I asked her, "Did anybody tell you anything? Have you heard anything?"

She said, "No! Nobody told me anything. My heart tells me the truth."

"What does your heart tell you, Mom?"

"You don't live with him anymore. You are separated, and my baby is heartbroken," she replied.

I burst into tears. I couldn't stop myself. I could not pretend anymore. I told her what happened to me. I told her everything, and I said, "I didn't want to upset you. I didn't want you to cry. I didn't want you to feel worried about me. I told everybody not to tell you."

Instead, she said, "I am happy for you."

I was shocked, hearing that from my mom. I thought she would be so devastated to hear her daughter's life had been wasted.

She said, "If he was that kind of person, you are better off without him. This is a big sin! You should not live in a life where there are devil's actions. You should get away from that dirty marriage."

I didn't know what to say. I thought maybe I didn't know my mom at all! I didn't know how open-minded she was.

She said, "I pray for your peace of mind. I pray for your son, and I will curse that husband. I will pray he gets whatever he deserves. I will ask God to punish the person who broke my innocent, pure, and kind daughter's heart."

The divorce happened very soon after. Because of the law of infidelity, we did not need to wait for a one-year separation. After almost four months of living in limbo, we divorced. My son left the house. He didn't come back home. I grew lonely, desperate, and experienced all the stages of grief, anxiety, depression, and anger at the same time.

The man I now called ex-husband was not in a better place, either. He tried to reach out. I closed the doors and all the contact possibilities. I blocked him from everything. He could not reach me. He tried to leave notes at my car window, but I tore them apart! I did not want any contact. I did not want to look at his face or see any sign of him. I did not know how I would have reacted if I saw him again.

Others said things were happening so fast for us, but it seemed like it took forever. It seemed to me like ages that I waited with this broken heart, but others were right. It was just a few months; why did it seem like a century?

My son came to say, "Let's try another amicable contract between both of you. You are both adults, do not fight!" He had tried helping us before, but that was unsuccessful. He wanted to give it another try. He was hurt as much as I was. His soul had been damaged, too. I knew he tried to support us. My son loved his dad and me and wanted us to be at peace!

I cried so hard again and again! My ex-husband came and knocked on the door, but I was not sure what to do! I sobbed and could not breathe. I decided that I would open the door. Through the half-open door, I could see that his eyes were red. He had been crying as well. I let him in. He sat on the floor, and we cried together.

He sat on the floor while I sat on the couch. He grabbed my feet. He cried so hard, and I tried not to look directly at him. I watched the TV playing sad music.

He said, "I know I hurt you so badly. I know I was stupid. I was blind; what I did was very wrong. What I did was unforgivable, but can you please give me another chance? I'll do everything for you. I'll be at your service."

I tried not to look straight at him.

In my mind, I visualized him sleeping with other women, hugging them, kissing them, and telling them he loved them while I was at work, while I was alone at home. I felt trapped. It had been four months that I felt trapped, devastated, and lost. It had been four months that I experienced all the stages of grief: anger, denial, depression, and acceptance. I was finally at the stage of acceptance. I tried to accept what happened to me and my 30 years of marriage. I looked at him briefly and decided not to say anything.

I kept trying to understand, but even from the other perspective, it never made sense. If you are a man, don't be selfish. If you don't see her as a masterpiece, let her go. If she doesn't excite you as before, let her go. If your heart doesn't beat faster when you see her entering your arms, let her go. Someone else would die for that. If you don't love them anymore, don't hold them back. Don't be cruel to them by holding them hostage and not letting them know what's going on in their real life.

Could I give him another chance? I needed to heal. I needed to decide for myself. For four months, I cried nights and days. I was not able to sleep at night. I had not eaten properly for four months; I had not laughed or smiled.

He put his head on my feet, and he cried hard. I couldn't stand it. I could not see him crying.

I said, "I curse those women who go after a married man. I curse those women who build their homes on someone else's castle."

It's a pity how some women try to build their castles by ruining someone else's dream castle. It's more pity and shameful a man would let that happen. Of course, these relationships are not permanent, and as a famous proverb says, "the moon never stays behind clouds."

He asked me to forgive him, and I said I'd try. Maybe not today, but one day.

A Dream of My Late Mother-in-law, Who I Love Dearly

After separation, I still thought about my husband's family, especially my mother-in-law who died when my son was only 2 years old. I saw her in her flat. A big family album was open in front of her. My sisters-in-law were there too. It looked like they were listening to our conversation but pretending to be busy with other stuff in the other corner.

"I want to remove that picture of mine from the album if you don't mind..." I told her softly, standing in front of her.

She looked up, and I saw sadness in her eyes. "But you are in this photo with us."

"I know, and from now on I don't want to be... please take it out of your album."

She put her soft, chubby hand inside the album and took out that picture of me, her son, herself, and my sisters-in-law. Then she hesitated, looked at me again... I saw agreement along with regret.

She handed me the picture, and I said, "I'll be a part of your family from a distance..."

I woke up... and wondered why my face was wet.

If I could go back in time, I'd tell myself this: Everything happens for a reason; you might not believe it in your crises but there will be better plans for you waiting. Be patient and trust the power of the universe and karma. Get professional help during crises, even if you must borrow money for it.

Cry when you need to, scream like no one is around (I ended up doing it while driving with my music loudly playing in the car, so no one would hear me.) Talk to your trustworthy friends. Do not believe all of them. Evidently, one family I trusted and cried my eyes out before them betrayed me by telling the cheater our confidential conversation word by word — their justification was to prevent the divorce.

Even though this is not medical advice, I'd tell myself this as it helped me: You can go on antidepressants only for a short time... this is PTSD, not depression. You will not be able to sleep or eat for days and nights! Go with prescribed sleeping pills for at least two weeks... talk only to trustworthy people who won't judge you or misguide you.

I eventually left home for almost a month, since being in the same house with him was giving me anxiety, anger, and frustration... do it if it helps you.

Chapter 10: Sama Whirling Dance for My Son's Engagement

Today was Thanksgiving, a beautiful and warm day. I danced with my son at his engagement party. I had practiced this dance for hours; while rehearsing, I imagined myself thriving in love. I followed every move, every figure, and now was the time to present it. I danced with a broken heart twisted by betrayal and separation. This should have been the happiest day of my life and we should have been celebrating this day with our little family: me, him, and his dad, but someone was missing.

The wedding planner had done a great job. The decoration was so luxurious, harmonic, and colorful. Dining tables were adorned with white and pink roses and embellishment of Persian foods, turkeys, and candles. The traditional Persian matrimony table, the *Sofreh Aghd*, had a beautifully crafted design. The tea serving table, dinner, and dessert, everything was well presented; everyone was impressed. It looked perfect.

Despite all the beauty here, my tears rolled down, blurring my eyes. I couldn't even see my son and his bride properly since the tears blocked my sight. I had forgotten all the moves that I had practiced for so long. For a few seconds, I had even forgotten the song lyrics.

Where was I? I was in front of my most favourite person celebrating his special day. My handsome boy was getting married. He looked at my eyes while dancing and sent me a kiss. My heart was filled with love, happiness, and sadness at the same time.

I muttered a Persian song called "A Dreamy Night," from Aron Afshar. "You are all I have wanted. You just ask and I'll surrender all my life to you. I love you forever."

I searched for my son in my memory. A tiny little baby handed to me for the first time. I tasted the real flavour of motherhood with him on a snowy Valentine's Day. I remembered the day he started crawling and the moment he stood up on his feet for the first time. We were in Mashhad at my sister's house, and he was only 13 months old. He stood up, and we were trying to hide our excitement when we saw him walking... one step, two steps, three, four, five... My heart was going to stop anytime, six, seven, eight steps. There was a butterfly in my stomach. Nine, ten, eleven, twelve, thirteen steps, and he gave up and fell.

Then there were happy screams and clapping from my sister. We all rushed to hug my son. The clapping at the engagement party brought me back to where I was. Here, it was him with his beautiful bride, sending kisses to me.

I recalled the first day of his school when I insisted, he go to school with a suit and tie in grade one, not knowing that was forbidden... and here he was now in a groom's suit. I recall the days I dropped him off at school and tried to kiss him. He tried to disappear soon so his classmates wouldn't see me kissing him. Now, I hugged and kissed him and his bride with all my love.

I looked at his kind eyes and remembered his first day at university when he was a well-mannered young man and tried to be independent. Twenty-seven years of us living together and building memories with each other floated through my memory during this one-minute song. We had celebrated these moments with the family of three of us. That was a bitter song of my heart, which had been shattered into pieces. I caught my son's eyes and our eyes locked on each other. A lump in my throat had been stifling me and we both started crying. Only two of us knew the deep meaning of these tears; but then I tried to get back to my happy world and engulf myself in this song.

My son was always there for everyone in his life, even people he had met for the first time. When you touch strangers' souls and make a difference in people's lives in a better way, someone one day will do the same to you. By spreading good, good comes back to you. He had found his soulmate.

My tiny little boy, I was so happy for him. I wanted to focus on this moment, on resuming our life with our new member of the family. I wanted to be grateful for what had been left; to welcome our bride to this family. I felt I was not here, though; I was not on the earth. I felt I was somewhere else, somewhere above, somewhere beyond. I was not myself. I was free; I was beyond the place and time; I was beyond myself. I didn't belong here.

It is so amazing how our brain works. It was a lesson and reminder to close off all negative thoughts and bad vibes. Why? What's in the word we tell ourselves? There's energy in our words, our thoughts, and our actions, which we must be mindful of. We can shift our sadness to our magnificent moments of happiness, and we shout out our livelihood. I was still alive, and this moment was for us to celebrate. When I finished dancing, I looked around and I saw tears in the crowd's eyes, people who knew our story, our friends who had shared some parts of their lives with us.

Our friends told me later my dance looked like a Sama whirling dance. Sama, meaning the Universe, is a dance that allows the dancer to become centered with their inner spiritual world and thus be able to connect with the universe. It's said to be the dance Rumi performed while singing "*Masnavi*'s Poems."

When the groom and bride joined the party hand in hand, my heart was racing, and my hands were shaking. I was full of joy and happiness. My face was bright, my smile was big, and my eyes shone.

It was proof of some great power at work. Open your heart to the universe, be kind to others with no expectations. The universe gives you back the same.

I stared at them. They looked great together. My tiny baby was now a grown-up, handsome young man holding his bride's hands, looking into her eyes with love, appreciation, and honour. I looked at them and, from the bottom of my heart, wished for their happiness and a joyful life together. It proved to me two simple lessons.

One: no matter what happens, don't give up on being the true, honest, genuine, and authentic person you are.

Two: what you put into the universe; the universe gives back to you. My son gave love and care to everyone unconditionally and in return, he got the most beautiful love from his sweetheart with her kind and caring heart.

It was a small gathering, but it was magical. The smile on everybody's faces reflected in their eyes and warmed our hearts. We were all gathered to celebrate the beginning of the new life of this young couple. We were on the balcony facing the CN Tower. The tower watched us from the far distance; the sun shone, giving us hope and warmth. The bride's sister sang a passionate song about love. I was beyond happiness. I was joyful. I was fulfilled. But there was still an emptiness in my heart. You could find a trace of betrayal in there which still hurt.

My son's dad was not here. I was sure he had eagerly waited for this special day, but his actions had consequences. When he didn't want to remain one of us, not to be part of our family of three, we needed him to know that he was not invited into this happiness. He must be regretful and ashamed by now. Our three hearts were wounded. I was sure my son wanted his dad to be at his side on his special day. No one even asked where the groom's father was, but you could see they wondered. They didn't want to hurt our feelings, so they didn't ask.

Apart from this absence, every single person had so much fun. Love was in the air, and we could feel it, touch it, and breathe it. There was still so much to honour. We all deserved to be happy.

I called this Thanksgiving night the magical night. We were all connected as one, celebrating the unity of this young couple's souls. I repeated to myself that I was not broken; life still had so much to offer. I was ready to receive this beautiful Thanksgiving Day. I was whole!!

Chapter 11: I Set Myself Free, Florida Getaway

The speaker announced my flight to Florida; I needed to get on the plane. I was almost getting up to grab my carry-on, but my phone beeped. There was a message, "Sorry Betty, I can't accommodate you. Please find another place."

I couldn't believe what I had just heard. My friend whom I was supposed to stay with in Florida just sent this message. I had no time to answer. I thought to myself: *"Should I just cancel my flight? I would have no place and no ride there. I am not sure where to go."* That was my first time visiting this city.

In two minutes, I had to decide.

"Okay, no matter what happens, I am not going to stay on the street. Let's take this adventure. I'm going. I'm not giving this up. I will search for another availability and find a good place beside the water."

I was not even sure which area was the best; not sure where to book to be close to beaches. There was an old couple sitting, waiting for their flight announcement. They seemed cold and distant.

I approached the old man and asked, "Do you know which area is closer to the beach?"

It looked like he had a hard time hearing. Or maybe he didn't understand my accent. He said something irrelevant to my question and then brushed me off. I didn't give up.

I asked his wife, "Hi, it looks like you know Florida. This is the first time I'm going to visit there. I don't know which area is closer to the beach. I need to book an accommodation there."

I pointed at the map. "I'm going to book here. Is this close to the beach?"

She looked at me, surprisingly. "No, this is far from the beach. This is downtown - more like a historical district."

I said thanks and searched in the mobile app to book somewhere close to that area. I booked the first thing I found immediately without even reading the reviews or searching for other options. I was almost the last person to enter the plane. I found my seat and located my suitcase. I had some time to sit comfortably and think, but not much after liftoff. I felt a lump in my throat and burst into tears.

Flying out of Canada, I looked out at the cloudy sky. It was a gloomy early morning, full of sadness and tears. I didn't like it there anymore. Everything looked unbearable. The sky seemed threatening. It was chilly, and my heart was colder than this December day.

I remembered the day we landed in Canada, three of us; me, him, and our 10-year-old son. We were full of hope and couldn't wait to begin our life in this country. We arrived on a hot, sunny day in July. We finally built a comfortable life together through so many challenges and learnings. I still can't find any reasonable justification for how our small family fell apart. None of our accomplishments seem interesting anymore. He sucked out my energy. I wanted to be somewhere that he could not reach me; somewhere he could not see or touch me, he could not tell me he loved me or that he wanted another chance. I wanted to be far away. I wished I could close my heart and forget all the memories we built, but everything in Toronto reminded me of him.

Flying high above the clouds, I was absorbed in thought. The gentleman beside me tried to interrupt me. He was chatty and happy, but I was not. I didn't show any interest in the conversation, and he finally gave up. Every passenger seemed happy with a big smile. They were all running away from cold December to a warm and sunny destination. Shortly, the plane passed through the clouds, and I didn't see anything else from the window. All I wanted was to stay there inside the white, fluffy clouds on top of Florida's sky forever. I wanted to live inside that cloud eternally. I didn't want to see anything else anymore.

My shoes hurt me, so I removed them. When I fly, they do not fit anymore. Then I remembered my nightmare. Now, I am not afraid to be barefoot. I do not look for my shoes anymore. I wished I could run on those fleshy clouds and get lost there. Now, running barefoot gives me a sense of freedom. I don't belong to a fake marriage. No matter if he was sorry and regretful. No matter if he asked for forgiveness. The damage was done. I was not related to him on paper anymore. I was not his wife, but only the mother of his son. My life would be different now. I needed to learn about my new identity and live like a single mom from now on.

It took a few seconds, and the plane pulled itself out of the cloud, and I felt disappointed since I couldn't travel through the clouds anymore. But I grew excited when I saw the blue sky again. The sun was shining, and I mumbled: "I am not broken. There is hope at the end of the tunnel." When I left Toronto early that morning, the sky was cloudy and gloomy; it had been snowing in Toronto for the last few days. In Florida, it was all sunshine and blue sky, warmth, and heat.

I closed my eyes and pondered. I needed this; I had to be gone. This getaway was much needed.

When I landed, I didn't know anything about living in Florida. I had never been there before. I just knew I came to hug the sun and get kissed by sunshine. My mind wandered again. I was not in the clouds anymore. This had become the reality of my current life.

Did I feel empty, void, unloved? Deep down, I still felt miserable. Hope was a far reach to dream. Yet, I tried to be optimistic. I needed to rebuild whatever he killed in me, my hopeful feelings, joy, and my passion for living. I was exhausted. How could I gain my strength again? How could I be happy and joyful again? I closed my eyes, telling myself, *"Let's leave it and surrender it to God."*

I took a taxi to the island and got to the boat house I had rented. On my way, I asked the driver to stop at the grocery shop. I did some grocery shopping; I bought foods and snacks, and then I went to the boat house. It was a beautiful place. My window opened to the *Caloosahatchee* River. I could see the sunset from the rooftop of the boat. There was a gorgeous patio to sit and enjoy the sunset, looking at the boats and ships coming along. One girl joined the boat a bit later, and a young couple came along in the evening. There was a bar behind our boat house; people chatted, laughed, sang, and danced there. Americans were happy, especially in warm and sunny states. A young guy who helped me find the boathouse worked in that bar and asked me to join him for a drink that night. I said maybe, but I didn't want to go. I was not in any mood to drink with anyone. I don't know; it might have been fun, but my heart wouldn't let me go.

Later, I thought about how I was far away from my home, from him, from the house that recently reminded me of women I didn't know sleeping with my husband in those bedrooms. Women who walked into my kitchen, looked at my garden, and spent time with him in our house. This would kill me someday. How much longer would I be reminded of this past? These feelings bothered me for the last six months, and I was not sure if they would ever leave me alone at all. I was shattered and heartbroken; I was not myself anymore. His affairs killed all of us, killed the trust and love.

Our beautiful house was being sold! Some other family would come to live there; they would love the house and the garden we built bit by bit. They would see the yellow and white daffodils and colourful tulips in April. They'd be surprised by our beautiful purple and pink lilac trees, which would bloom in May. All summer long, they'd enjoy our various hydrangeas and red and pink climbing roses and the garden beds surrounding the big and beautiful gazebo, which my husband assembled and worked hard for. They would enjoy the wooden flower beds he made, and I had planted every year with different colourful begonias and geraniums.

This new family would love the kitchen. We designed it carefully together and made hundreds of different delicious dishes there while he helped me by chopping the vegetables carefully and meticulously. We threw countless parties and family gatherings in this living room; New Year, Christmas, Thanksgivings, Easter, Norouz, birthdays, and more. How many dances happened in this beautiful house while the happy dance music was loudly cast through a sound system on the ceiling? All was gone in the blink of an eye... I couldn't love this house anymore; I couldn't live in a place where betrayal happened, where I was lied to, and where strange women enjoyed it in my absence.

I was certain the new buyer would have a happy life in this house, which was built with love, care, and kindness. *"Damn you, husband! You ruined everything. We immigrated all the way here to have a better life. We all went through hell to be here, and you ruined it. Damn you... I may forgive you someday for the sake of our 30-year life together, for the sake of our good times together, but I do not forget, and I will not come back to you anymore."* I would gather all my broken pieces and build myself again.

Finally arrived

Florida was warm and sunny. I got a taxi, Uber, sitting at the back of the taxi looking at tall old palm trees! There was sun shining over it. How warm and peaceful this is. The driver is quiet, a very handsome and polite man. I said, "I need to do some grocery shopping on our way." He looked at me in the mirror, as though he didn't understand what I just said.

"Yes restaurant!!!" he replied.

"No, I'm not going to a restaurant. I want to do some shopping, grocery shopping."

"Okay!!" he said, but I was not sure if he understood me.

"Where are you from?" I asked.

His eyes shone when he replied, "Cuba."

"Oh, you speak Spanish?" I asked.

His eyes sparkled brighter. "Yes!"

I tried to Google and find a proper sentence in Spanish: "I'm going for grocery shopping." I found the translation and showed him on my mobile.

He read it, then he nodded yes and said, "Compares de comestibles." I smiled.

He searched through his phone and showed me a picture of a beautiful Spanish girl dancing and smiling. He also showed me a video of her dancing in Rome, Italy.

"She is gorgeous, and she looks very happy," I said.

"She is my daughter. She is a dance instructor in Italy," he said with pride, in broken English. Then he looked at me in the mirror. "She is *preciosa*."

"She is *preciosa*," I repeated.

"*Preciosa*" in English means lovely, gorgeous, precious.

He shuffled through the pictures on his mobile of his wife and grandchildren.

I thought to myself: *"Here in Florida, they can drive and use the phone at the same time?"*

His phone was on a standing device in front of him. He drove and at the same time shuffled the pictures and videos.

"I am 54 years old," he said while exchanging pictures.

"You have a very young heart. You are lucky to have such a beautiful family."

"I have been in Italy for 20 years. My son was a doctor back then, but here in the States he works as a nurse," the man explained.

"I am also a nurse."

We chatted all the way to my resort. He also talked about his birthplace and the lifestyle in Cuba. I tried to talk in Spanish using Google and he tried to practice his English.

He took me to Walmart. While I was shopping, he waited outside.

I was at the cashier when my phone rang with an automated call from Uber: we noticed your taxi has had no movement for the last 10 minutes. If you are in danger, press one, otherwise press two.... I laughed and pressed two!

I gifted him a package of dark chocolate. He had a call from Uber as well, asking why he stopped. I appreciated the system. He looked at my bags of groceries.

"I am not planning to stay here forever."

"Women!!!!" he said, while nodding his head and then we both laughed.

He dropped me off at the address of the boathouse and left with a warm hug and goodbye. I wished him all the happiness in the world.

I looked at the building and had no idea if I was in the right place. It looked like I was not exactly at the boathouse but a few metres away. I took my carry-on and my bags and started climbing the stairs, wondering how I was supposed to carry this heavy stuff with me. Then I saw a young white man standing on the balcony. He had blue eyes, white skin, with rosy cheeks. He was tall and slim, wearing shorts and a white sleeveless top.

"What do you think you're doing, girl? Do you think this is a hotel?" His voice had a heavy southern accent.

I looked at him, then realized I had my cashmere top with my jeans on in this hot sunny weather. "You can tell I'm coming from a cold place. Look what I'm wearing."

"Let me help you." He grabbed my bags. "You got a lot of shopping."

I smiled.

"It's hard to get there. You need to step on the rocks with those heels." He pointed out my shoes.

"I can manage, I guess!"

"I golf today. Do you golf?" he said while taking me to the boat house.

"I would love to try, but I have never done it."

I didn't know how to thank him enough for his help. I loved the boat house. "*This will be a different experience,*" I said to myself.

He dropped me at the door; I knew the code to open my room. I thanked him again.

"Would you like to join me for a drink at the bar?" he politely asked.

"I'll try," and then I went inside.

There was a young, beautiful Spanish girl cleaning the kitchen. I was in shock. She was maybe 17 years old, and she was very pretty. I introduced myself. She was very warm and nice.

"I'm sorry. I'm going to make a mess here with all of my groceries."

"That's fine. Let me know if you need anything. My job is done. I'm leaving now," she said.

On the last day of my vacation, I would give her the foods and fruits that I couldn't finish.

The whole boathouse was mine at that moment. Nobody else was there yet. It was gorgeous. I thought to myself, "*Everything happens for a reason.*" It was good that I had to book this place at the last minute.

On this beautiful island, I would have a chance to take a rest for a while and collect my energy. There was only me to look at the sunset and meditate. I needed to find myself and embrace my new identity. I was ready to surrender myself to destiny. I stretched my legs and looked at the window with the river view. How cool was this? I had never travelled alone, only gone back home by myself. I couldn't wait to enjoy the scenery and be hopeful about the future. It was a great gateway to plan for whatever I always wished for. I had no other obligations, and I could decide on my own life.

Again, there were better plans for me waiting. I didn't believe in it while I was dealing with my crises for months. But life showed me more opportunities. I decided to be a travel nurse since I wanted to do this from the beginning of my career, but my family was my first priority. Now I could achieve this dream. Soon I started travelling to different places, hospitals, and cites. New people, new culture, and new me. No one in these new workplaces knew about my wounds. It was much easier to deal with those wounds alone and be away from the place where I was wounded. Memories were getting pale, and events weren't as harsh and terrible looking as before. I could see the depth of events; I could analyze them and search for the cause. Now I am a life coach and know more about relationships and their challenges. Now I am able to help myself and repair my broken wings and be the complete butterfly I always wished for. It seemed at the time I broke into pieces but now I know for a fact that I'm not broken.

Be adventurous! I could easily have cancelled my flight because my accommodation plan was cancelled right before the flight. But I took a plunge and booked the first available booking. I am not regretting, since the new plan took me somewhere unexpected!

Acknowledgement

This book, and the contents within it, would not have been possible without all the incredible people who helped me on my life's journey.

My mother is a woman who exemplifies strength and principle in all she does and gave me the foundation upon which I built. To her, I owe my gratitude, love, and life for making me who I am today.

To the light of my life, my son, Abteen. For always inspiring me with his kindness, his heart, and love for humanity.

To my dear friends and family, I owe many thanks for their continuous and unconditional love and support throughout my life journey. For being my guardian angels, lifting me up when I felt down, and their gentle reassurances as I built and re-built my life, piece by piece.

To my daughter-in-law: Anosha *Amin* for helping me translate the introduction and one of the forewords. I'm eternally grateful for all you've helped me accomplish. What had started out as a simple idea became a beautiful accomplishment, which would not have been possible without your contributions. It is because of your guidance, love, and support that this book is sitting in our very hands today.

To my readers — you are all the very reason I wrote this book. This book would cease to exist entirely without each one of you. Thank you for the opportunity to tell you my story and thank you for taking the time to read it. May your own stories live on, adding yet another piece to the beautiful masterpiece created by all of humanity that is called life.

Special Thanks to My Publisher

Most importantly, I want to thank my author coach and publisher, Pantea Kalhor, who helped me, step by step, to make this book happen. Pantea's experience and expertise were all I needed. Her encouragement and patience with every step I took is much appreciated. When I was down and couldn't continue writing, she was there to lift my spirits up and helped me not give up. Her excitement was no less than mine, if not more… her enthusiasm and longing for this memoir to be published gave me the strength to continue.

About the Author, Betty Khalili

Betty was born in Tehran, the capital of Iran. She came into the world as one member of a big family, with pillars built on strong religious principles. Her family was just one of many in a middle-class neighbourhood.

She finished her schooling in Tehran and went to Shahid Beheshti University of Medical Sciences for her undergrad in Nursing.

She got married and moved to the north of Tehran, *Shemiran*. She and her family lived there for 11 years. They had their only child there. The family of three moved to Toronto, Canada in June 2004. She pursued her passion and took complementary educational courses in Canada and eventually started working as a nurse in downtown Toronto.

Later on, she got into the aesthetic sciences and began working in a clinic for a number of years. Her life took a drastic turn when she went through a divorce, which led her down the writing journey, getting her started in writing her memoir, all while obtaining her life coach certificate and working as a travel nurse.

Me in different stages of my life

My son Abteen in different stages of his life

Our memorable backyard and family gatherings

My adorable mom

My beloved family

My Sister Atefeh and her note on her room's door in Farsi: *It is what it is, we can't change our destiny.*

CPSIA information can be obtained
at www.ICGtesting.com
Printed in the USA
BVHW060523081022
648923BV00003B/335